1

FEAR AND LOATHING

in the

LONE STAR STATE

by

E. R. BILLS

2021

Fear and Loathing in Texas

Fear and Loathing in Texas © 2021 E. R. Bills

Trade Paperback ISBN: 978-0-578-95644-2

Cover Art: *Captain Texas* (2021)
Artist requested anonymity.

PR1

Maybe they ought to lock the people up in the bank vaults and let the money doing the living.

—Philip Atlee, *The Inheritors*

FOREWORD

Faster than the will of the people. More powerful than the minority ballot. Able to skip over considerations of fairness and justice with the stroke of a pen.
    LOOK!
Up on the pink granite floors of the capital!
It's a birdbrained Trumper!
It's plain miscreant! It's . . . It's . . .
Captain Texas.

 Jade Helm invasion? *Call Captain Texas.*
    Concerned citizens protesting an oil and gas pipeline running through their back yard? *Call Captain Texas.*
    Women exercising sovereignty over their own bodies? *Call Captain Texas.*
    The Electric Reliability Council of Texas (ERCOT) dropping the ball in the ice storm last February? *Call Captain Texas . . .* and he'll build a wall.

In the bizarro, comic book version of the Lone Star State, Red numbskulls run things, and Greg Abbott is their hero. And for a smarmy, vacuous climber, he's hell on wheels.
    Despite the title, this collection is not an example of Gonzo journalism, but it does offer Gonzoism. Harsh jabs, relentless barbs and dead-on editorial commentary—which can be both useful and terrifying. Simultaneously.
    I could just as easily have borrowed the nomenclature for this collection from Kierkegaard's *Fear and Trembling*, but trembling doesn't quite capture sentient folks' reaction to the good ol' boy cluster-frack that we currently find ourselves in, much less the wholesale ignorance that allows it to thrive. If I'm harsher on "Captain Texas" and his cohorts than their hapless counterparts, it's because the worst aspects of our state were fortified on their watch. George W. Bush, Rick Perry and now Abbott.

Texas isn't a good place right now, and Texans are not headed for bigger and better things. In fact, it's exactly the opposite. We've become a small people governed by our own worst angels.

We don't even trust ourselves with the truth.

E. R.
07/16/21

CONTENTS

The Party of "Abortion" in Texas

Fort Worth Weekly June 2, 2021

It's ironic that Republicans in Texas are so committed to abolishing abortion.

Abortion is their primary *modus operandi.*

Abortion is basically their chief reason for being.

Every election season, Republicans try to abort voting rights, especially for Texans of a different complexion. And, as much weeping and gnashing of teeth as Republicans do about late-term abortion, they would gleefully abort the results of the last presidential election. An inordinate number of Texas Republicans tried on January 6th. It's just who they are.

While the United States of America was established by the descendants of immigrants, the Republic of Texas was actually founded by immigrants. There were only two native Texans who signed the Texas Declaration of Independence (their names were Jose Francisco Ruiz and Jose Antonio Navarro), so, naturally, Republicans are fierce opponents of immigration and naturalization. Republicans would abort immigrants if they could, but, in recent years they've had to settle for separating immigrant children from their parents and placing them in cages along our border. It's sad, but at least these kids are brown.

Texas Republicans aren't real keen on persons of color—immigrant or no—unless they're carrying a football. Which brings to mind another white conservative conundrum. It's difficult for Texas Republicans to think highly of themselves or their forebears if the facts about Texas independence and the countless atrocities committed against persons of color are widely propagated. Truth-telling, therefore, must be aborted. It's a constant priority. But—to their tremendous benefit—the only thing more powerful than white fragility in Texas these days is conservative white political agility.

When Texas Republicans aren't obsessing over ways to disenfranchise persons of color, they go after women. Texas Republicans have a perpetual, Viagra-esque hard-on for aborting women's reproductive rights, and also fight against fair pay for Texas women. It's no wonder there are less and less Republican babies around.

And there's the real rub.

White women have the most abortions. If women of color were the largest demographic utilizing birth control or terminating their pregnancies, Texas Republicans would make birth control and abortion kits available at the drive-thru of every Whataburger in the state.

There's no reason to mince words.

Texas Republicans initially aborted the insurance exchange clause of Obamacare here in the Lone Star State to poison the proverbial well. It denied millions of folks affordable health care and, ultimately, killed Texans just to score political points. More recently, Texas Republicans aborted the right to protest Big Oil and regularly abort clean air and clean water measures, poisoning millions of Texans, destroying animal habitats and restricting access to precious natural resources. And Texas Republicans are currently working to abort reasonable gun control efforts, abort real reforms of the Texas power grid (which killed Texans in February of this year) and abort the homeless (instead of mitigating the conditions that create them).

16

Oh, and Texas Republicans get away with all this because they helped abort the FCC Fairness Doctrine back in 1987, ushering in a media environment where a propaganda machine like Fox News could brainwash conservative voters, convincing them to self-abort theretofore long-standing notions of honesty, conscience and human decency.

In a word, Texas Republicans are more of a miscarriage than an abortion—of justice, of intellect, of forethought and of reasonable governance. But abortion is the means by which they simultaneously make our state a laughingstock and a menace.

"Captain Texas" is trying to build more walls along the Rio Grande. I'd say he's handicapping the wildlife in the borderlands we share with Mexico and sending out the wrong message about who Texans really are.

No Boundaries

Fort Worth Weekly January 13, 2010

On the morning of December 28, 2009, I woke to a big surprise. My tent and the ground outside it were covered in snow. And it was still coming down.

The day before, I had hiked into the Chisos Mountains of Big Bend National Park under sunny skies and fifty-degree weather. I had hoped to reach the South Rim but, at 7500 feet it got dark on me and I had to camp. I pitched my tent at the elbow of a switchback and, then, to avoid attracting any critters, stuffed my food items into a bag and tossed it up into a tree about fifty feet from my campsite.

The snow the next morning worried me. How much more would there be? Would it make the trails and passes dangerous? I decided to exit the Chisos Basin and head back down. I packed up my tent and retrieved my foodstuff.

The snow on the trail was completely fresh, and I appeared to be the only traveler in the silent Basin wonderland. There was no sign of another living creature for the first half hour of the hike.

I'd forgotten moments like this were possible, especially sitting behind a desk. Taking orders, giving orders. Buying, selling—being bought and selling out.

The silence of the trail was like the glass of windows I stared out when I was daydreaming. I saw some of the things I had been missing and the possibilities I'd dismissed and forgotten. There, all around me, in the mountain air and prickly Chisos brush, I felt alive and vital in a way I hadn't in years.

At the trail turnoff for Juniper Canyon, I was reveling in the moment and still amazed that I was alone in nature and part of it. Then I spotted something that broke the spell. There in the fresh snow was an animal track, the foot pad about three and a half inches in diameter with five small toe prints on top. The impression was fairly fresh and the print was the first of several heading in the same direction as me.

It was a black bear, probably 200- or 300-pounds, and it was somewhere ahead of me. The print was mind-blowing and unmistakable.

The black bear is endangered in Texas; they had all but disappeared from the Chisos Mountains until bears coming up through Mexico re-established the species. I—we—had encroached on the black bears' habitats for years, practically leaving them no place to live. But, thanks to their Mexican kin, they were back.

I was glad nature knew no borders.

When I settled into a warm motel room that night, I thought about the bear prints and started weaving a clever, satirical piece around the idea of almost stumbling into a furry, 400-pound illegal alien that the federal government was currently welcoming into this country with open arms and spending our tax dollars to support and protect. I thought I would blame the exorbitant cost of our healthcare system on him and complain that, despite the good things one could say about the bears, they were still here illegally and utilizing our social services without paying taxes or learning to speak English. I considered using the bear as a humorous vehicle for mocking the ignorance and hypocrisy that clouds our views on immigration.

But I just told the story instead.

Back on the trail, I took a break and let the bear be on his way. I never saw him, but, thankfully, he also never saw me. I was the alien there, and he was the native. I was sure his policy on newcomers was more humane than ours, but I didn't want to push my luck.

He was much better as a bear than as an allegory. And I liked sharing the world with him.

The fact that former educators bristle at talk of removing or dismantling Confederate monuments says a lot about the education levels of Texas voters.

Take 'Em Down

Fort Worth Weekly March 7, 2018

At an appearance I did the other day for the Texas Retired Teachers Association-Eagle Mt.-Saginaw Retired School Employees, I faced a doozy of a final question. A woman asked me what my take was on the Confederate statues being taken down around Texas.

Prudence was never my strong suit, but I warned her, suggesting that I was probably the wrong guy to ask. The crowd waited for my response.

Here it is.

They say history is written by the victors. Evidently, they haven't been through the South.

In the South, history was written by the Losers, and the Losers are still crying in their spittoons about the outcome of the Civil War, about desegregation (except on the football field), and about the debate over their Loser flags and Loser memorials.

Yeah, yeah, sure. When I was growing up, I admit I enjoyed Clint Eastwood's *The Outlaw Josey Wales*. But that was before Clint and I realized the author of the book on which Josey Wales was based was not (as originally stated) a Cherokee writer named Forrest Carter but actually Asa Earl Carter, a former Alabaman Ku Klux Klan leader and speechwriter for George Wallace who assumed a new identity when he moved to Abilene, Texas.

What's that? You say members of your family fought bravely for the Confederacy? Fine. Great. Their heroism and fierceness may be unparalleled in the annals of American military history. But they risked their lives, lost their lives (or limbs, wholeness, sanity) for folks behind an institution and an ideology that presupposed a group of human beings who looked different than them were not human, not deserving of basic human rights (or dignity), and not worthy of being treated with any pretense of basic human consideration, decency, or conscience. Which simply puts your relatives in the company of all the Germans who fought bravely for the Nazis in WWII.

What's that you say? Your forebears didn't own slaves? Ah. Now we come full circle.

Your forebears were no different than American soldiers today. Most were patriotic rubes duped into a fool's errand for rich white men. Contemporary U.S. soldiers sacrifice their lives, limbs, and psychological wholeness for corporate unscrupulousness and the perpetual United States slot machine that is the Military-Industrial-Complex. And that's one of the reasons so many of them are committing suicide.

In most cases, American soldiers are not off somewhere defending this country (or our freedom), fighting the good fight (if there is such a thing), fighting against legitimate enemies, or fighting for anything resembling jokingly noble intent. And when they get back on American soil, this lesson is increasingly hard to stomach.

There is no question that the men and women in our armed forces today are fighting fiercely and bravely, but they're not fighting for causes or objectives that are worthy of their sacrifice. They're fighting for lies—just like our ancestors who brandished weapons under the Stars and Bars.

At the end of the day (and this argument), that's what Confederate monuments symbolize: a time when soldiers were duped into fighting for an ill-intentioned aristocracy with no concern for human justice or being on the right side of history.

Here in Texas, we actually threw our own George Washington—Sam Houston—under the bus when he warned us that secession was a mistake and refused to sign off on our idiocy.

Like all the Texans who refused to fight for or support the Confederacy during the Civil War, Houston was a real rebel and a real hero. Not a fool, a dupe, or a Loser.

I say dispense with the Lost Cause theology. I say take down the Loser flags and the Loser memorials.

If you were whistling Dixie around these parts before, during or after the Civil War, you lost, and you plainly and inarguably deserved to lose. And the less we see of your inhuman cause and your Loser symbols, the better.

I remember when Republican gubernatorial candidate Clayton "Claytie" Williams likened bad weather to rape, advising that "If it's inevitable, just relax and enjoy it." The quip helped get Ann Richards elected in 1991, but three decades along, Claytie—an avid Aggie oil and gas man now deceased—gets the last laugh.

Condoms Optional: Getting Fracked by the Oil and Gas Industry in North Texas

Dissident Voice October 20, 2010

I chuckled out loud the other day when I heard that a "No-hooker" zone in Arlington was rejected by the city council and Mayor Robert Cluck. I know Arlington Police Chief Theron Bowan's request for this exclusionary section was an earnest attempt to address the prostitution problem that has sprung up around Rangers Ballpark and Cowboy Stadium, but the whole measure was pricelessly ironic.

If you look up the meaning of the verb form of "prostitute" in the dictionary, you'll find two definitions: 1) to sell the services of oneself (or another) for purposes of sexual intercourse; 2) to sell oneself, one's artistic or moral integrity, etc., for low or unworthy purposes.

We like to forget that second denotation in Capitalist society. It hits too close to home. Who are we to question the system? Who are we to question how other folks' livings are made?

The problem with not asking these questions in our community is that we also like to believe that criminality is punished and justice is at least striven toward.

Prostitution is illegal and I have no problem with Chief Bowman or the City of Arlington accosting, arresting and prosecuting hookers in what's come to be known as "prostitution central" in the city's entertainment district; but it's like chasing a pimply-faced, emo drop-out with a ½-ounce of pot down a dark alley instead of seizing a drug cartel kingpin in broad daylight.

The biggest whore in Arlington is not an abused, down-on-her-luck junkie, trying to fund her meth habit. The biggest whore in Arlington is Republican Congressman Joe Barton.[1] Since early 2009, he's been the U.S. House of Representatives' biggest recipient of contributions from the oil and gas industry, approaching $2,000,000 in "love" money. And he's loved them long time.

Barton has been in on or led every attack on repeated federal and local attempts to regulate the pollutants that the oil and gas folks are pumping into our atmosphere and our water supply and, at the height of the BP Spill hearings, he even apologized to former BP president Tony Hayward for having to endure the criticism and grievances aired by fellow congressmen who don't put price tags on their virtue or conscience. And now, if the Republicans retake the majority in the House, that beady-eyed little strumpet will be trying to sell his "wares" as Chairman of the House Energy and Commerce Committee.

But the Arlington cat house offices of Congressman Joe Barton are not Tarrant County's only den of obscene wantonness. Of the approximately 43,000 zip codes that make up these United States, the 76102 zip code of downtown Fort Worth leads the nation in political contributions from the same high class clients that pimp Barton: the oil and gas industry.

Regular 76102 "Johns" include XTO Energy, Chesapeake Energy, Range Resources, Titan Operating and Quicksilver Resources, and over $250,000 in "love" money has made it into federal coffers from this area in this election cycle, $225,000 of which was given to the oil and gas industry's favorite "escort," the Republican Party.

I don't know about you, but where I come from, a quarter of a million dollars pays for a whole lotta' "fracking." And that's what the lechers downtown are paying for. They want to drill the Barnett Shale cheaply and discreetly, and they don't want the going rates for the "tricks" they enjoy raised or the mess they make fussed about. They like a "Wham-Bam-Thank-You-Ma'am!" arrangement that allows them to get in and out without attracting too much attention.

So I don't want to hear about Arlington police officers rousting small-time hookers around Cowboy Stadium unless some version of a federal vice squad is going to shake down Barton or give the "Johns" of 76102 the Hugh Grant treatment.[2] They operate the biggest rings of prostitution in our community.

"Bartleby" is still dead and his murder by the Haltom City Police Department has received no further media coverage to date.

Bartleby Is Dead

Fort Worth Weekly June 20, 2020

Though we had worked for the same company for two years, I didn't know him very well. He kept to himself. I don't know what he thought of me, and I wasn't exactly sure what to think of him. He was just a guy who came to work, almost like Melville's scrivener Bartleby.[3] In fact, that's what I'll call him for now. Bartleby.

I got the impression that life had not been easy or very kind to Bartleby, but he was always easy to deal with and kind to me. And always respectful. His father died not long after he first came to work with us, and in the last year or so, his best friend passed as well. He had a daughter who was attending a local college, and he was very proud of her—but I didn't know her name. He preferred bowling to golf—on that, we both agreed. Neither of us was really "frat boy" material. Oh, and Bartleby had a nice smile. We didn't see it often, but it was nice. Beyond that, I didn't know much about him.

Last week, however, I heard something that I couldn't process. And I didn't hear it from him.

Bartleby was in the Intensive Care Unit at John Peter Smith Hospital. He'd had open-heart surgery, and half his skull had been removed to relieve the pressure on his brain. One of his eyeballs had been shot out. He might never recover. He might never wake up.

News stories said four Haltom City police officers responded to a "shots fired" report in the 2300 block of McGuire Avenue. In the middle of their "response," Bartleby "came around the corner of McGuire Avenue and Nina Lane" in his grandmother's compact sedan. It's been said that Bartleby stopped in the middle of the road—presumably when he saw the Haltom City police cars—and yelled at the officers. It's also been said that he then went to his trunk and took something out of it. According to the *Dallas Morning News*, "Authorities didn't specify what the item was."

Finally, it's been alleged that Bartleby got back into his grandmother's compact sedan and began "driving toward the officers." Four of the Haltom City police department's finest opened fire on Bartleby. He was struck by several bullets, and it's been said that his grandmother's compact sedan veered into a telephone pole. But in the pictures, at least, it looks like it rolled to a stop at the nearest curb.

I'd like to see the dashcam or officer camera footage of the incident.

Even though Bartleby and I weren't very close, I'd like to know what really happened. Bartleby wasn't a gun nut. Bartleby didn't strike me as a troublemaker, much less a cop killer. In fact, he didn't seem the least bit confrontational—even when others were confrontational with him. On top of all that, he'd just gotten a raise and seemed genuinely thrilled.

The newspaper and television reports almost suggest a scenario that resembles the last sequence in *The Vanishing Point* (1971), where the antihero protagonist barrels full-speed into bulldozer blades the police have lined across the street to stop him. But I don't believe it. Bartleby was just a guy I worked with.

What it seems like is that Haltom City cops responded to a "shots fired" complaint and found somebody to shoot. I suspect that is the story behind the headlines that the Haltom City police dictated. The problem for them, I think, is that Bartleby lived on Nina Lane. He was probably leaving his house to run an errand or trying to return to his house after visiting a grocery store. I don't think he had any idea what he was driving into.

Bartleby is dead now. His funeral date isn't set because this man the police assumed was dangerous, driving down the street in his grandmother's compact sedan, was an organ donor.

That news doesn't surprise me. That's the kind of guy I think Bartleby was.

Bartleby was the last person I ever expected to perish in a hail of gunfire. In fact, I think if I'd have asked him if he would have liked to be mistaken for a threat and gunned down in cold blood by the Haltom City police on Memorial Day weekend, I am certain he would have responded just like Melville's Bartleby. I envision him saying calmly and politely, "I would rather not."

Bartleby's name was James Milligan, Jr.

We like to think of ourselves as Davids, but we're the nation of Goliath. Just ask any of the eighty foreign countries and territories we keep military bases in.

We Are the Beasts
Fort Worth Weekly April 14, 2010

In many ways, Hunter Layland was like any other freshman boy in the Metroplex. He played football, spent time with his friends, and tried to adapt to high school. But unlike most young people learning the ropes in our communities, Hunter didn't have much luck. He'd been in a car wreck as a toddler, and it left him with facial scarring and hearing problems. At Cleburne High School, he was constantly made fun of. Some of his schoolmates even went so far as to say that if they looked like him, they would kill themselves.

On September 31, 2009, at 6:35 a.m., Hunter did exactly that.

Over the last few months, I've thought a lot about Hunter and some of the kids who got bullied when I was in school. Some of them had it pretty rough, but most of us hardly even noticed or cared. I think about the scorn and derision they endured and how, even though I wasn't party to it, I certainly didn't do much to prevent it. I was too concerned with being cool or popular, or simply deferring to the bigger kids.

I remember the victims' names and faces. I even remember what was said to them and about them. They were targets of ignorance, stupidity, and sheer meanness. They were often teased unmercifully no matter what they did. And, like Layland, their attempts to placate their tormentors only made things worse.

Looking back, I can't help but despise myself a little for not doing something. I could say it wasn't any of my business or my fight. But that doesn't help. What happened to some of these kids should have been everybody's business. We were all to blame.

As I get older and re-examine the events of my life in broader perspective, it's not always the things I did that give me painful pause. It's often the things I didn't do, like not speaking up when I should've or not standing up when others were being pushed down.

This summer will mark the 25th anniversary of my high school graduation. Out of my class of about eighty-five kids, only two have died—and both committed suicide. One killed himself while we were still in school, the other a few years ago. I hardly knew the former and certainly wasn't a friend. I knew the latter well enough, but we had our differences. I don't remember either of them as being obvious marks for bullies, but they didn't have it easy either. And when I read that another kid at my old high school committed suicide this last fall, I couldn't help but think of them. And Hunter Layland.

I don't know how some of the kids we mistreated had the fortitude to keep coming to school. The slights, the name-calling, the trip-ups. There wasn't a lot of room to breathe. And there certainly wasn't any room to be different.

The most shameless tormentors in my school back then are normal folks today, happy, complacent, and churchgoing. Did they finally achieve enough popularity or a strong enough sense of superiority to erase the need to bully? When they get down on their knees to pray at night, do they beg forgiveness for what they did to kids like Hunter?

In my experience, our victims usually don't attend class reunions, and, if they do, they seldom betray any hard feelings. Did that which didn't kill them make them stronger?

What is it in so many of us that craves superiority, that requires us to put down others to feel better about ourselves?

31

We seem to need victims, pariahs—collective or individual otherness that we can rally against or look down upon. In fact, it often seems like that's where we're most comfortable.

I hope Hunter is at peace now, in a place where scars and misfortune don't make him the target of human knavery. I'd like to think he didn't die in vain, but the news indicates otherwise. As long as folks are still showing up at town hall meetings with guns or threatening people whose ethnicity, belief system, or appearance are different, then the bullies are still at it. And we're still not stopping them.

Will the Buc-ee's beaver finally become the official symbol of Texas?

A Real Alamo

Fort Worth Weekly June 16, 2021

I get it.

As a native Texan, I feel your pain.

I, too, was weaned on comic book versions of the Alamo and the Texian War for Independence, and I understand your anger and frustration. We have been betrayed.

The question, now, is what are we going to do about it?

Should we slap AK47s over our shoulders and strap pistols across our beer bellies and stage our own Alamo about what never really happened at the Alamo at the state capitol? Do we need to stand tall with the Texas chapter of the Daughters of the Confederacy and protest these shameless revisions to all the lies we hold dear? Or is it time to face the Mariachi music?

Call me crazy, but I'm a proponent of the latter.

The genie is out of the proverbial Tequila bottle.

It's time to reckon with an ugly truth. Texas independence was mostly about slavery (and *gringo* knavery) and not much at all about bravery. In fact, the biggest things in this state chockfull of big things, are the whoppers we've told about our history for almost two centuries.

But, hey, on the lighter side . . . you have to admit . . . Ozzy Osbourne[4] is looking smarter all the time. And Phil Collins[5]—maybe he should *sue . . . sue . . . Sussudio* all those so-called Alamo relic peddlers.

I bet he feels like a real *pendejo*.

But fret not, fellow Texans. There was actually a real Alamo. Dozens of native Texans—not of the mostly white immigrant variety that fought in the fake Alamo, of course—bravely volunteered and voluntarily fought and died to preserve the freedom of a people and stop Spanish-speaking Fascists. It just didn't happen here. It happened in Spain, one hundred years after Texas independence.

In 1936, conservative nationalist Fascists attempted to topple the left-leaning government of Spain. Liberals, progressives, communists and anarchists came from all over the world to the defense of the Spanish Republic, but the Fascists were backed and supplied by Adolph Hitler and Benito Mussolini. Oh, and also a Lone Star oil and gas outfit known as Texaco. Texaco refused to sell oil to the freedom fighters, but allowed the conservative fascists in Spain to put the oil they imported for their insurrection on a tab until the war was over.

In hindsight, the Spanish Civil War was a dress rehearsal for World War II. And, while FDR and the United States remained neutral, thousands of Americans came to the aid of the Spanish Republicans, including dozens from Texas.

Needless to say, the good guys lost, and the leader of the Fascist insurrection, Francisco Franco, ruled Spain as a dictator until his death in 1975.

But, get this.

Conroe, Texas native Philip Detro rose to the rank of Commander of the Lincoln-Washington Battalion and hung out with Ernest Hemingway before succumbing to complications resulting from a sniper's bullet.

Fort Worth, Texas native Theodore Gibbs—a black man who ran away from his home in Cowtown at the age of thirteen after witnessing the rape of his mother by her white employer—joined the freedom fighters in Spain and drove an ambulance until he was killed by an artillery shell.

Laredo, Texas native Virgilio Gonzalez Davila served with the Washington Battalion and then transferred to the 46th Division *Campesinos*, a "shock force" who fought in every major conflict of the war.

Texarkana, Texas native Conlon Samuel Nancarrow emigrated to Mexico after serving with the Peoples' Army of the Spanish Republic, and went on to become one of the most original, influential musical composers of the 20th century.

And Oliver Law, a black native of Matagorda, Texas, became the first African American to command an integrated military force in American history. He was killed in action while leading Abraham Lincoln Battalion in the first days of the Battle of Brunete.

Dozens of red-blooded native Texans fought in Spain, serving alongside or hobnobbing with the likes of Langston Hughes,[6] George Orwell,[7] Paul Robeson,[8] Federico Garcia Lorca,[9] Pablo Neruda,[10] Andre Malruax,[11] etc., etc.

Sure, they were a bunch of liberals who thought for themselves—and fought for someone besides themselves—but they were still Texans. And they went to fight in a real Alamo, for freedom and human rights—not the preservation and expansion of a disgraceful travesty.

That's something, right?

God botherers bother me. They're Christianity's worst ambassadors.

The 10 Commandments: Shouldn't We Try Living up to Them Before We Demand They Be Posted?

Dissident Voice January 9th, 2010

A half dozen times a year I see headlines regarding some conservative group's attempt to place a Ten Commandments monument at their local courthouse. It reminds me of those "I Support the Badge" decals that speeders put on their back windshields. It doesn't mean they'll be traveling through life any safer or kinder. It just means they think they have an "in" with that Big Patrol Officer in The Sky.

There are many religions in the United States and to allow the proponents of one to place a memorial at a public facility, without allowing all the others to do so, would obviously be discriminatory. But I might be inclined to entertain such a request if the adherents of said faith even jokingly attempted to abide by their own moral decrees.

Ambrose Bierce[12] once defined a Christian as "One who follows the teachings of Christ in so far as they are not inconsistent with a life of sin." At the dawn of the 21st century, it would be hard to refute Bierce's assessment, and even harder to deny American Christendom's abandonment of the Ten Commandments.

Commandment I indicates that we shall have no other gods before God and we arguably don't. Unless you count money, celebrity, beauty, professional sports figures or the newest hit at the box office. On a daily basis, they all receive more reverence than the Holy Spirit.

Commandment II tells us not to make or observe false idols. The fact that we make gods (or demigods) of radio, screen and sports stars and prostrate ourselves in front of the TV each week to venerate the grace of *American Idol* or *America's Next Top Model* makes this commandment falsely idyllic.

Commandment III instructs us not to take the Lord's name in vain, i.e., misuse it, profane it or otherwise sully it via human mischief, malarkey or deceit. So when corporations begin peddling piety and godliness to sell products or politicians begin invoking God's name or intent to win elections, they sin unequivocally. There's hardly a politician alive or dead who didn't wrap him or herself in old time religion to get elected, but the previous White House occupant [George W. Bush] transmogrified it into a campaign platform, claiming God told him to run (There's a special pitchfork for him to sit on in the afterlife, but we won't fare much better—we adored his sacrilege so much we elected him twice.).

Commandment IV says to remember the Sabbath and keep it holy, but when God was making the world He didn't have restaurants to go to or malls to shop in. Plus, football, basketball, baseball, golf and NASCAR hadn't been invented yet. If God was creating the world today, He wouldn't have paused on the seventh day to rest. He'd have stopped to watch man-children pointing up at Him every time they scored a touchdown, goal or basket, or hit a home run.

Commandment V instructs us to honor our mother and father. That's what shrinking Social Security checks and nursing homes are for, right?

Commandment VI forbids us from doing that which we do very effectively and perpetually. Kill. Abortion may be murder, but so is war, capital punishment, denial of adequate healthcare, credit card or mortgage indentured wage-slavery, pollution, etc., etc. We are killers. We kill in the name of justice. We kill for profit. And we kill to protect our insulated, superficial way of life. Amen.

Commandment VII regards adultery. Ouch. Christ said a man who ogles any woman besides his wife commits adultery. The *Bible* says divorce for any reason other than infidelity is adultery. Sex before wedlock is adultery. Porn is adultery. Politics is adultery. *Desperate Housewives* is adultery. Golf is adultery. What would Hollywood and the American advertising industry sell us *sans* adultery?

Commandment VIII addresses thievery. But Bill Gates'[13] ship came in when he basically stole the QDOS computer operating system idea from Gary Kildall[14] and leased it to IBM. Now he's the richest human being in the world, a philanthropist and all-around great guy. The moral of American Capitalism is the ends justify the means.

Commandment IX indicates that we should not bear false witness against our neighbors. But this is obviously the job description for the political pundits who tell us what to believe. Glenn Beck[15] and Rush Limbaugh[16] bear false witness for a living. Sarah Palin was recently honored with "Lie of the Year" for her "death panels" guile, and, for her transgression, she's garnered significant political traction and received millions for aspersion-mongering.

The final commandment condemns covetousness, so we, of course, ignore it. Good God-fearing Americans measure their worth and righteousness in terms of possessions. Materialism defines the human condition and the big wheel of prosperity stops spinning if people quit buying things they don't need. If we extricated covetousness from our socio-political process, wouldn't our entire culture collapse?

Obviously, before we mob the nearest courthouse to post our principles, it would be a good idea to try living up to them. If that's not possible, maybe we could just put them on a rear window decal.

Never know when that Big Patrol Officer in the Sky is going to have us on His radar.

Speaking of radar, the truth doesn't seem to be on ours. We have little or no interest in truth, especially if it makes us look bad or challenges the falsehoods we hold dear.

Critical Race History in Texas
Fort Worth Weekly July 7, 2021

In late December 2015, Constance Hollie-Jawaid and I were still working on the final plans for the dedication ceremony for a Texas state historical marker commemorating the Slocum Massacre. The fight to get the marker approved had been grueling, and, on that particular day, we had traveled to Palestine, Texas, to meet with the marker effort's chief antagonist, Anderson County Historical Chairman Jimmy Ray Odom.

Jimmy's beliefs about the Slocum Massacre were almost completely contradictory to ours, but—in conversation, anyway—he was a straight-shooter. Our historical and cultural disagreements notwithstanding, I respected him for that.

Jimmy had taken some heat in the press for his straight-shooting, and he was upset with me. And when we met that day in late December, he let me know this in no uncertain terms. At that point, however, the marker was secured. Constance—a descendant of victims of the atrocity—and I had won the argument, so we could be magnanimous. I let Jimmy air his grievances without response or complaint. In fact, even though the Anderson County Historical Commission had fought the Slocum Massacre historical marker application tooth and nail, I even agreed to write a short piece for the *Palestine Daily Herald* thanking Jimmy and the commission for cooperation that had been virtually nonexistent.

After the discussion regarding the marker ceremony concluded and the air was a hair more convivial, I asked Jimmy why there was no historical marker for a Black activist named Frank J. Robinson—and his response was as straightforward as it was shocking.

"Oh, they killed him," Jimmy said.

Constance's and my jaws smacked the hardwood floor simultaneously.

I had stumbled across Frank J. Robinson when I was writing *The 1910 Slocum Massacre: An Act of Genocide in East Texas* (2014). He had known Abe Wilson, one of Constance's forebears on her father's side, and the man whose appointment to round up black and white citizens for county road repairs in the area at the time had infuriated a half-renter named James Spurger. Spurger would become the chief instigator of the Slocum Massacre.

Frank J. Robinson was a daunting force for good in Anderson County in the 1960s and early-to-mid 1970s, mentoring Boy Scouts, volunteering for church youth groups, and constantly advocating for equal civil and voting rights for minorities all over East Texas. To these ends, he eventually organized the Anderson County Civic League, which encouraged Blacks in the Palestine area to run for public office.

No African American had ever held public office in Anderson County, so the all-white commissioners court gerrymandered the county's voting precincts, diluting the Black vote by dividing it into three separate parts. Robinson subsequently created the 16-county East Texas Leadership Forum so African Americans could combine their collective resources to challenge and procure judicial redress. Then, with the support of the ACLU, the AFL-CIO, and other progressive organizations and individuals, Robinson and two other plaintiffs sued the Anderson County Commissioners Court.

On March 15, 1974, a district court sided with Robinson et al., stating that the Anderson County precincts were racially apportioned and ordered the county to redraw the lines. Anderson County appealed the decision to the 5th Circuit Court of Appeals, and the ruling was upheld in December 1974. The changes Anderson County was required to institute led to the election of the first Black public official in East Texas history, and African Americans in several other East Texas communities followed Robinson's lead.

But Robinson didn't stop there. In short order, he organized the East Texas Project and initiated litigation aimed at making the City of Palestine address the ways in which its election system disenfranchised minorities, but the work didn't get very far. On October 13, 1976, Robinson was killed by a shotgun blast that the Palestine authorities ruled was self-inflicted. Expert witnesses, including a Texas Ranger who testified that no gunpowder residue was found on Robinson's shirt, challenged the official determination, but the ruling of suicide still stood.

And then I matter-of-factly asked Jimmy Ray Odom about Robinson 40 years later, and his response was unequivocal.

Oh, they killed him.

Throughout my research and work on the Slocum Massacre and the Slocum Massacre historical marker, I was repeatedly asked why it was important to bring attention to something that happened over 100 years ago. *Why were Constance and I stirring up trouble? Why did what happened then matter now?*

Well, Frank J. Robinson—a civil rights champion who basically delivered democracy to East Texas for African Americans—was probably assassinated for his efforts in many of our lifetimes and most of us have never heard of him.

Isn't this type of history critical?

41

Neither the War on Drugs nor the War on Terror have been as lethal or effective as the War on the Middle Class. And our leaders wage it without a lick of conscience.

Wrong War

Fort Worth Weekly October 5, 2011

My father grew up on Gordon Avenue on the South Side of Fort Worth. After high school at Trimble Tech, he apprenticed in the construction industry and became a journeyman electrician. In the 1970s he earned an average of $40,000 a year.

It was a fair wage, a good wage. The average price for a new home was $50,000. The average price of a new car was $4,500. Gas was fifty-seven cents a gallon. A bottle of soda pop ran thirty-five cents, and you could get five or ten cents back if you returned the bottle. Being an electrician was a great way to make a living.

Today, the average journeyman electrician still makes approximately $40,000 a year, but the average price for a new home is $100,000 and the typical price for a new car is $20,000. Gas is about $3 a gallon and soda pop is $1.75 a bottle. Working as an electrician is no longer a great way to make a living.

The wages for many of the blue-collar, middle-class jobs in construction, manufacturing, and the service industries haven't changed much in the last 40 years, but the prices for what they build, produce and service have tripled and quadrupled.

Why does everything cost so much more even though the folks who are doing most of the actual work don't make any more than they did 40 years ago?

Well, it's obviously complicated. The price of the materials has risen along with cost of the fuel required to transport goods. Then there are higher insurance costs and, in some cases, pension plans. But a significant percentage of the increase of the costs of products, goods and services in general can be traced to folks who do very little if any of the actual work. I call them the CEO or MBA class.

While wages for so many of us have remained stagnant, theirs have increased by a thousand percent or even more. Where they used to earn ten times what the average man or woman on the line or in the field used to earn, many of the fat cats now make hundreds of times what that worker earns. And their salaries continue to increase as they break up unions or ship our jobs overseas.

The well-heeled apologists for these new robber barons would have us believe that middle-class unions and blue-collar collective bargaining rights are the reason the price of everything except our wages has gone up—but the real reason is the class they serve. Corporations have to pay our executioners—*I mean their executives*—well. Their steely lack of conscience is invaluable. They keep boards of directors happy and never let common decency or antiquated notions of loyalty, shared struggle, or fair play get in the way of the bottom line.

It no longer pays to be a craftsman; it's more important to be crafty. Pride in your work isn't profitable; quantity trumps quality. Every Wal-Mart in America is a testament to middle-class expendability. Where there were once millions of mom-and-pop shops, where the employees knew your name, there are now thousands of big-box shops where Mom and Pop earn minimum wage as "greeters." The individual items we buy there are cheaper, but our collective quality of life is also greatly cheapened.

Tomorrow, you and I will be earning the same or less while the CEO/MBA class steals more. Their kids will coast through the finest private schools and expensive universities, while ours will be lucky to graduate from intentionally understaffed public schools and even luckier to struggle through the only colleges we can afford.

How long will the sparsely privileged meekly accept the world according to the agents of their own disfranchisement? How much longer can we afford to elect these upper-class lackeys? What's it going to take to stop us from kissing the hands that slap us?

The Republicans of late have taken to accusing President Obama of class warfare. Can they not see that the middle class has been suffering in the trenches of class warfare for years?

Any CEO who makes hundreds of times more than the man or woman doing the real work has middle-class blood on his or her hands. Any CEO who allows manufacturing jobs to be shipped overseas is spilling blue-collar entrails. And every big-box store that monopolizes Middle America digs a thousand blue-collar graves.

Class warfare has been waged against the middle class for years. It's time our assailants faced the consequences.

Trumpers make Bush's "Clarion-ettes" look like editorial staff of the Harvard Law Review.

Earth To Bush Loyalists: Unwavering Faith Won't Save Us (Or You)

Dissident Voice June 11th, 2007

On a September evening in 1956, Marian Keech claimed she received a message from a planet called Clarion, instructing her the world would be destroyed by a catastrophic flood on December 21st. A middle-aged woman living in the American Midwest, Keech[17] also said the message informed her that several flying saucers from Clarion would come and rescue her and those close to her before the apocalyptic deluge.

Mrs. Keech's revelation attracted and inspired a small group of ardent followers. They quit their jobs, gave away their money and abandoned their houses. They withdrew from friends and family and, in some cases, left their spouses. Then, they waited for December 21st.

On the morning of December 20th, Mrs. Keech said that she had received another communication from Clarion. She announced that she and her followers would be picked up at midnight, and that they should make sure there was no metal in their clothing or attached to their person when the transport arrived. Her followers complied, removing all metallic clasps, zippers and buttons from their clothing.

When midnight came and went, the group became anxious. Through the early morning, they began to succumb to lapses of doubt and despair. By 4:00 a.m., they sat in stunned silence.

But just when the gravity of their mistake had begun to sink in, Mrs. Keech received another message. The inhabitants of the planet Clarion informed her that rescue saucers would no longer be coming because the planetary cataclysm had been diverted by the unwavering faith of her small group of believers. Mrs. Keech and her followers rejoiced and began spreading the good news.

To the outside observer, Mrs. Keech's followers appear to have been incredibly naïve and gullible. But consider the alternative. If Mrs. Keech was a fraud, then they had quit their jobs, gave away their money, abandoned their houses and cut family ties for nothing and, perhaps, worse than nothing, a lie. Their lives would be ruined and they had nothing to show for it. But if they had saved the world, they were part of a miracle and had earned the ultimate mark of distinction. Believing this, they could reconcile the loss of familial relations and worldly possessions. They were simply sacrifices made for the sake of saving the rest of us.

Mrs. Keech's followers remind me of contemporary Bush loyalists. During the dinner circuit of his 2004 presidential campaign, Bush once said his base was comprised of the "haves" and the "have-mores." Today his base is made up of the "ignores" and the "ignore-mores"—folks that have invested too much of their energy, enthusiasm and integrity in supporting Bush and now can't (or won't) admit that they were wrong, that they were lied to, that they promoted lies, defended lies—that they have politically embodied a lie for the last seven years. The evidence is all around them, but they refuse to face it.

Support for the Bush administration began tailing off after the Abu Graib scandal[18] and the Valerie Plame leak,[19] but after investigations into pre-war intelligence determined that there was no pre-war connection between Saddam Hussein and Al Qaeda and that there were also no WMDs in Iraq, Bush's approval ratings nose-dived and never recovered. Subsequently, staunch "Bushies" no longer enjoyed the pseudo cover of righteousness and patriotism or the audacity afforded to them by an obsequious, muzzled press corps. They found themselves in an awkward-leaning minority, and the rapid public opinion shift resulted in substantial 2006 Congressional mid-term election losses for their party. Suddenly, in a country where "W" decals once adorned the back windshields and bumpers of every other car and truck on the road, it was hard to find any.

Now, as the war (or, better said, our occupation) in Iraq drags on and on, the painful truth is that the entire fiasco was based on lies. Big lies. And the big lies were compounded by dozens of ludicrous, outrageous smaller ones, rhetorical calculations, facts spun, truths distorted: *Mission accomplished! The insurgency in Iraq is in it's last throes . . . They hate us for our freedom.* Etc. Etc. Etc.

The writing is on the wall, but, amazingly, Bush still retains the support of millions of die-hard, devout followers. And they're still repeating the party line from planet Clarion.

If Saddam didn't have WMDs, well . . . *we know* he was trying to get them.

If Al Qaeda wasn't in Iraq under Saddam, *uhhh* . . . well, they're there now and they must be stopped.   And they probably really were there all along.

It's just the liberal media twisting things around.
Freedom isn't free.
The rest of you just don't have the guts to finish the job.
We should just nuke them.

Like Mrs. Keech's group, loyal "Bushies" seem to be capable of believing anything to keep from admitting they were wrong. Confessing to the rabidity of their unquestioning support for Bush would cast them in an unflattering light. They can't face the facts, because doing so would require an admission of guilt, complicity and the cold blood they carry on their hands. They're like a desperate, hysterical cult that would rather drink red (as in Republican) Kool-Aid than own up to the untenable sins of blind faith, irrational allegiance and the strictly observed, almost regimental ignorance that brought us to this unconscionable quagmire.

But, unlike Mrs. Keech's followers, Bush loyalists have no chance for a "happy" ending. The war in Iraq will not be won. And their faith in Bush and the Republican Party will not prevent Iraq from becoming an unsightly blotch on our national self-esteem for decades to come.

In the end, the unfortunate soldiers that went there to fight and lost their lives or their limbs or their buddies or their peace of mind will have done so for nothing or, again, worse, lies. American lies. Bush's lies.

I wish flying saucers from Clarion would come down and make our mistakes in Iraq disappear or go away. But it's not going to happen. This time, unwavering faith doomed us to disgrace. And the sooner we accept it, the quicker the healing can begin.

After this piece appeared in Fort Worth Weekly, *I was emailed by one of Katie Couric's*[20] CBS Evening News *producers. They were looking for contact information for Sgt. Hale's family, because they wanted to do a broader discussion of this issue. I explained to him that my editorial was simply an opinion piece and I hadn't contacted the family. I don't know if Couric or* CBS *ever wound up doing a feature on Sgt. Hale.*

Johnny Got His Pills

Fort Worth Weekly October 27, 2010

After U.S. Army Sgt. Douglas Hale, Jr. finished fifteen months in Iraq for his second combat tour, it was obvious that things in his life had gone awry. In 2007, he was diagnosed with severe depression and post-traumatic stress disorder. He began drinking heavily and his marriage fell apart. In early 2009, Hale abandoned his post at Fort Hood. This past May, he was arrested for being absent without leave and returned to Fort Hood. Before the month was out, he tried to kill himself.

The Army sent Hale for treatment at a psychiatric hospital in Denton, and it seemed to help. He spent the 4th of July weekend with his mother and she drove him back to Fort Hood on July 5th. On July 6th, his mother received a text message from him that said, "I love you mom im <sic> so sorry I hope u and family and god can forgive me." She immediately contacted Army officials at Fort Hood and started driving back. But Hale had already shot himself in the head.

Our Army brass is looking for answers regarding the suicides of soldiers like Hale, but not under their noses. War is insane. It isn't hell; it's a planned, coordinated communal psychosis. If you take a normal, all-American boy or girl and plop them down in a psychotic situation for months and years at a time, tour after tour, psychosis or extreme disturbance are not abnormal responses. And they can lead to suicide. Especially when the nation who sent these men and women into harm's way still hasn't clearly justified why this madness was necessary. It's hard enough to maintain your sanity in a war zone when you're fighting the good fight. But when you're risking your life or limbs or sanity simply to fulfill the "wartime president" fantasy of an imbecilic, oil fund aristocrat or to enable a rich, pasty-faced assembly of stuffed shirts look "tough" on terrorism, your outlook on things isn't going to be positive. Or healthy.

I read an AP piece in the newspaper the other day that suggested that one of Big Pharma's wonder drugs was killing American GIs. It said that many of the soldiers serving in and returning home from the wars in Afghanistan and Iraq were taking a drug called Seroquel to help them deal with chronic restlessness, severe insomnia and constant nightmares. If I was a soldier it might have made me laugh.

Seroquel is a "potent antipsychotic." Instead of reducing combat tours to reasonable time frames, limiting the number of tours a soldier should have to endure or simply removing unstable soldiers from the psychotic environment of these ill-conceived wars indefinitely, the U.S. Military is apparently using our men and women in uniform as guinea pigs for a soldier's-little-helper pill that will supposedly desensitize them to the insanity around them.

It doesn't cure the psychosis. It simply allows unstable soldiers to function within the insanity without being terribly bothered by it. And when you combine Seroquel with antidepressants and anti-anxiety drugs—something military officials suggest is an acceptable "standard of care" for soldiers or veterans suffering from post-traumatic stress disorder—any semblance of normal sentience is truncated to the point where they walk around in a cognitive fog or detached stupor.

In this regard, isn't the U.S. Military's pharmaceutical attempt to abridge the humanity of our soldiers its own form of insanity? If you have to give someone a "potent anti-psychotic" to help them deal with what they're doing or what they've done for you or God or country—then there's obviously something wrong with what you're asking them to do. It is reminiscent of perhaps the grimmest excerpt from Erich Maria Remarque's *All Quiet on the Western Front*: "We were eighteen and had begun to love life and the world; and we had to shoot it to pieces. The first bomb, the first explosion, burst in our hearts."[21]

Conveniently, Seroquel is more than just one of the military's most frequently prescribed drugs. It's also the fifth best-selling drug in the nation. So if our psychotic naivete and ignorance ever start to really get to us, we can always knock them back with a brain-fuddling stupefacient. In fact, we've already been at it.

In 2008, American emergency rooms treated a million people for abusing prescription drugs and over-the-counter medicines, roughly the same number of folks our ERs treated for heroin and cocaine overdoses or abuses of other illegal drugs—and this number doesn't even factor in alcohol. We're taking the edge off our insanity any way we can. The only war more stupid and psychotic than the one in Iraq was the one on drugs. But it's been going on so long its mention no longer even penetrates our daze.

The military-pharmaceutical complex is making a killing or, more specifically, making a fortune off the folks we've asked to do the killing—and the rest of us. They dope our unruly kids, they dope the young men and women fighting in and returning home from the war; and they dope the rest of us right here at home for being sick of wars overseas and fearful of war on the Middle and Lower Classes and disgusted by Capitalist expediency and dreading the reckonings to come and being ashamed of our own sad, national shadow.

I wrote this after the Oklahoma City bombing in 1995. It could just as easily have been written after 9/11.

In the Aftermath

The Shorthorn April 25, 1995

To terrorize is to dominate or coerce by intimidation, the threat of violence, or the calculated perpetration of destruction, catastrophe, assassination, murder, etc. In the popular mind, terrorism is qualified by additional connotations. People recognize it as a vicious, cold-blooded attack on defenseless civilians or bystanding innocents. Few crimes are judged with such an unchallenged sense of vehement righteousness. Perpetrators of terrorism are hounded with unparalleled sanctimony and fanatic zeal. I read President Clinton's pledge in the newspaper: "Nobody can hide any place in this country; nobody can hide any place in this world from the terrible consequences of what has been done."

Indeed, I think . . . *unless they are American.*

Reports of the Oklahoma City bombing shock, enrage and sadden me, but an ancient adage haunts my conscience. *Those who live by the sword, die by the sword.*

For the last four decades, the United States has perpetrated terrorist activities around the world. Our remorseless handiwork in Vietnam, before and during the war, provided a chilling catalogue of American terrorism. The CIA-planned and CIA-executed assassination of the democratically elected president of Chile, Salvador Allende,[22] evidenced a harrowing propensity for terrorist realpolitik. And the United States has repeatedly installed and/or subsidized puppet dictators around the world who perform terrorist acts on their own constituencies.

On a subtler level, in cases such as Israel and, until recently, South Africa, we support governments that permit, if not directly sanction, terrorist enterprises against their own indigenous populations, ranging from summary executions to simple violations of the most basic human rights (Israeli terrorism is no doubt reciprocated by factions such as the PLO, but does that excuse it?).

I see tattered infant-victims of the bombing in Oklahoma City and cringe, rueful and angry. But my jaw also stiffens as I recall the Guatemalan and Salvadoran "Death Squads," the genocidal military wings of regimes we encouraged and assisted in rises to power in central America.

In Guatemala, we supported the coup and eventual overthrow of democratically-elected president, Jacobo Arbenz.[23] The faction we bet on—and invested in—began an incomprehensible reign of terror, decimating more than 440 indigenous villages, conducting an estimated 100,000 political killings (more than 40,000 called "disappearances") and leaving more than 200,000 children orphaned. And our man in Chile, General Augusto Pinochet, upstaged his Guatemalan counterparts, employing tortures that included inserting sabers in vaginas and disemboweling female victims while their families watched.

And who can forget the "fraidy-Eighties"?

No one in Nicaragua.

Men, women and children no different than the citizens of Oklahoma City were afraid all the time, and not just over one incident, but several every week. Besides funding and arming the Contras, we also published a terrorist handbook for their training. The CIA called it a "Freedom Fighters Manual," but included, among other things, detailed, illustrated instructions for making and utilizing Molotov cocktails.

These are just a few of the incidents where U.S. involvement in terrorist activities became public. There were no doubt countless others. In fact, by popular definition, the largest single terrorist achievement in human history was the allied firebombing of Dresden, Germany in World War, II. Although it occurred in wartime, it was a vicious, calculated attack on a virtually defenseless civilian community.

The second and third largest acts of terror in world history were probably our nuclear offensives in Japan. These incidents pale in comparison to the widespread genocides conducted by Hitler, Stalin, Mao Tse-tung and Spain and the Catholic Church (in South and Central America), but genocide is not an act of terrorism—it constitutes a regime or regimen of terrorism (of which our nation could be accused of in terms of much of the Third World in general).

As Americans, we are largely unaccustomed to terrorist bloodshed. But for much of the rest of the world, it's nothing out of the ordinary. They live with it every day.

I shudder at the scenes from Oklahoma City. But I also quake at our bloody ignorance. Did we think our acts of terror would never be reciprocated? Or that our fellow citizens were incapable of them? Did we really think we could be immune from terrorism after having so long been one of its chief contagions?

*The January 6, 2021 U.S. Capitol insurrectionists also had nothing
on the citizens of Grayson County in May of 1930.*

Michigan Has Nothing on Texas

Dissident Voice May 9, 2020

The "good," gun-toting white goons who recently protested safety measures necessitated by COVID 19 at the Michigan state Capitol had nothing on "good" white folks in Sherman, Texas ninety years ago today. They burned down their own courthouse to get at a black suspect, and then burned him as well.

On May 9, 1930, a 41-year-old African American man named George Hughes was asphyxiated and then burned to a crisp in Sherman, Texas.

According to reports, Hughes had moved to the area from Honey Grove only a few months before. He had worked on various farms and was then employed at Ned Farlow's place approximately five miles south of Sherman.

By late April he had grown frustrated with Farlow over back pay. At 10 a.m. on Saturday, May 3, Hughes apparently stopped working the fields and headed to the Farlow residence carrying a double-barreled shotgun. A neighbor called the Grayson County Sheriff's Department (from a nearby cotton gin) and Deputy Sheriff Bart Shipp responded. By the time Deputy Shipp arrived, Hughes had left the Farlow home and was walking into an alfalfa field. When Hughes spotted Deputy Shipp's vehicle, he fired on it twice, one shot going through the windshield. Deputy Shipp emerged from his vehicle uninjured and, as Hughes's shotgun was empty, arrested him.

It is unclear what transpired at the Farlow residence, but it can be assumed that Mrs. Farlow was alone and Hughes made an ill-advised visit to address unresolved issues of unpaid wages. Whatever occurred, Hughes was later charged with criminal assault. One account suggested Hughes had bound Mrs. Farlow's hands and feet with bailing wire; another report stated that Hughes had sexually assaulted Mrs. Farlow.

Due to the volatile nature of the charges, Grayson County authorities had Hughes transferred out of the county jail for his own safety. On Tuesday, May 6, a white mob attempted to retrieve Hughes and law enforcement personnel confronted the vigilantes, firing into the air to warn them off. District Attorney Joe Cox appeared and informed the mob that Hughes was not in the facility, but the mob was distrustful and requested that Cox allow a mob "committee" to search the jail. Cox acquiesced and the committee was unable to find Hughes.

After the mob's first attempt to seize Hughes, Grayson County authorities contacted state officials and requested assistance from the Texas Rangers. On May 7, Texas Ranger Captain Frank Hamer,[24] Sgt. J. B. Wheatley, J. E. McCoy and J. W. Aldrich left Austin at 4:25 p.m. and arrived in Sherman that evening.

On March 9, Hughes's short-lived trial began and the events that followed are best conveyed by eye-witness participant, Captain Hamer:

> *On the morning of the 9th of May the negro was brought into the court room. The jury was empaneled, the trial proceeded to get under way. It was while the first State witness was on the stand testifying, that the crowd made a rush on the District Court room to get the prisoner and in their attempt to do so, two double doors opening into a hallway near the District*

Court room were broken down. The District Judge [R. M. Carter] *ordered the prisoner locked up in the District Attorney's* [second-story] *vault and then we immediately proceeded to disperse the mob, which we did by use of our guns, without firing, and tear gas bombs. The District Judge and other officials then decided that a change of venue should be ordered in the case. The crowd made two other attempts to rush the court room on the second floor and was beaten back each time. I instructed my men that the next time they rushed the courthouse that I would fire on the mob, but for them to hold their fire until I gave orders to shoot. In a few minutes the mob attempted to rush the court room again, coming up the stairways and I fired a shotgun loaded with buckshot, wounding two men, so it was reported to us, this stopped the mob. I had heard a number of them say prior to the time that I fired on them, that 'you can't shoot us.' It never occurred to me what they meant until a newspaper man came up stairs and showed me a message that he said he had received over the A. P. wires reading as from the Governor, 'protect the negro if possible, but do not shoot anybody.' I informed him that I had received no such message, however, at this time, this report seemed to have been well-circulated among the crowd.*

I saw the District Judge and told him about this report and informed him that I didn't believe the Governor would issue such orders, because we probably could not hold the prisoner if such order was issued. One of the agitators walked to the foot of the stairway and asked me if I was going to give the prisoner up to them, I told him we were not, he says 'well we are coming up to get him,' I said 'any time you feel lucky, come on, but when you start up the stairway once more, there is going to be many funerals in Sherman.' For twenty or thirty minutes, things were quiet. They started breaking windows down stairs, the sheriff and deputies had previously gone down stairs, leaving myself and men to guard the negro and the stairways, then all at once the flames from the lower story of the courthouse swept up the stairways and on up to the ceiling over our heads to the second floor and myself and men barely escaped the burning building. The flames cut us off from the vault and we could not have opened the vault if we could have gotten to it, as we did not know the combination, so we came out and down into the crowd.

When the mob was unsuccessful at taking custody of Hughes by force and then couldn't get Captain Hamer to relinquish custody of him, vigilantes threw gasoline into the basement or somewhere along the first floor and ignited it. As squadrons of the Sherman Fire Department arrived and attempted to fight the conflagration, members of the mob held them back and severed their fire hoses.

When three hundred National Guardsmen (sent by Governor Moody) arrived to assist the Rangers in getting the situation under control, the mob—which had grown to number in the thousands—and Guardsmen clashed in pitched battles. As the Guardsmen were vastly outnumbered and generally disinclined to fire on American citizens, they suffered dozens of injuries and were forced to retreat to the county jail and fortify it to protect themselves and other members of law enforcement personnel.

The mob eventually learned that Hughes had been placed in the District Attorney's large, second-story vault and set about laying hold of him. By 4 p.m., the courthouse was gutted but the vault was still standing. The mob repeatedly, but unsuccessfully placed dynamite (utilizing ladders) to open the vault door and then employed it in conjunction with cuts to the outer casing by an acetylene torch. Later that evening a blast finally blew in the vault door and Hughes was discovered unconscious (one account indicated that part of his head was smashed in). Hughes's body was dropped down one of the ladders and struck the ground with a dull thud.

Members of the mob tied a chain around Hughes's body, affixed the chain to an automobile and dragged him "down to niggertown." The gruesome cavalcade ended at a tree near a two-story office building which housed several African American businesses, including a drug store, a beauty shop, an undertaker and a tailor. Hughes's body was hung from the tree by a chain and vigilantes piled up boxes underneath it. The mob set the boxes on fire and then burned down the African American office building. A reinforcement of Guardsmen arrived at approximately 2 a.m. and the mob dispersed.

On Saturday, May 10, images of the mob, the riot and the courthouse fire appeared in newspapers across Texas and the nation. Just after dawn, the Rangers and Guardsmen cut down Hughes' remains and sent them to a white undertaker (as the African American undertaker's parlor had been torched) and then sought out the hundreds of Sherman's black citizens who had fled into the surrounding thickets, hidden under homes or otherwise taken refuge. The Guardsmen transported them back to the African American section of the community. According to the *Fort Worth Star Telegram*, "not a negro was seen in the town from 2 p.m. Friday until Saturday daybreak, although Sherman claimed a negro population of 1,500 to 2,000." When the returning African Americans and their escort got back to their neighborhood, they discovered typewritten ultimatums warning black citizens to leave the city within twenty-four hours.

Fifteen suspected mob participants were arrested and several injured National Guardsmen were transferred to a Dallas hospital. As further rioting was expected, state officials ordered additional Guardsmen to Sherman and these reinforcements were supplemented by almost fifty law enforcement personnel from surrounding counties. A Fort Worth contingent, for example, was ordered to protect the main school and church in the African American section of Sherman and set up machine gun positions at vantage points on streets leading to these locations. Guardsmen prohibited white citizens from entering black neighborhoods without specific, approved reasons.

The *Telegram* would later refer to the rioting the night before as an "orgy" of violence and destruction, and Sherman Mayor J.S. Eubank [Though a Grayson County native, Jessie Shain Eubank (January 20, 1884 – June 7, 1942) was mayor of Corsicana from 1923-1925 before he served as mayor of Sherman.] would blame it on outsiders, claiming "Sherman has been made a victim of circumstance."

At 10:45 p.m. on May 10, Governor Moody declared a state of martial law after noting that "reputable citizens and officers of

Sherman, including Judge B.M. Carter, have reported to me that the mob threatens to form again," further endangering the safety and security of the community.

By May 11, Guardsmen were posted with machine guns at the county jail and every corner of the courthouse square. They began patrolling the city and forbade the congregation of more than three citizens at a time on any city street.

On Monday, May 12, a military court began conducting a probe into the rioting, gathering testimony that would be used when the Grayson County grand jury convened the following week.

On Tuesday, May 20, the grand jury indicted fourteen suspects in seventy counts of five separate offenses, including rioting, rioting to commit arson, utilizing explosives to commit arson, rioting to commit murder and burglary of the courthouse—no one was indicted in the death of George Hughes.

The Sherman citizens charged were Jimmie Arnold, C.E. Briggs, Leslie Cole, Jeff (Slim) Jones, Jim May, J.B. McCastland, Alvin Morgan, Horace Reynolds, Bill Sofey and Cleo Wolfe. Four other men from Van Alstyne were charged: Roy Allen, Leonard (Baldy) O'Neal, Web Purdom and Jess Roper. The bond for every suspect was set at $5,000 and their cases were transferred to Dallas County for trial.

On Saturday, May 24, martial law ended at 12:00 noon and the Sherman rioting suspects were transferred to a Dallas jail. On May 27, federal charges alleging a civilian attempt to disarm national guardsmen was filed against Sherman residents John Edwards, Will Hamilton and Floyd Sheppard and Waxahachie resident John Simmons, each man's bond being set at $2,000. Hamilton and Edwards immediately posted bond and the officials of Grayson County filed a $100,000 insurance claim on the courthouse even though the policy the county carried on the courthouse contained a disclaimer invalidating recompense in the case that the edifice was destroyed by rioting.

On June 23, 1930, Dallas County District Court Judge Charles A. Pippen denied a plea to reduce the bond set for the Sherman riot defendants and postponed the trial until September. By early

September, ten of the riot defendants had posted the $5,000 bonds, leaving only Arnold, McCasland, Morgan and Wolfe in Dallas County custody. On September 10, Judge Pippen announced that the hearings for the Sherman riot defendants would commence on September 29. On September 26, Judge Pippen postponed the hearings until November because the Grayson County District Attorney was busy with several other cases.

When the Sherman riot trial began, Defense Attorney J.A. Carlisle filed two separate motions to postpone the case again and transfer the hearings back to Grayson County. Judge Pippen overruled both motions and then had a disheartening encounter with an ugly Dallas County mindset.

Of the sixty-eight prospective jurors interviewed for the trial, sixty—almost ninety percent—declared openly that they would not convict the defendants even if the State demonstrated their guilt beyond a reasonable doubt!?

Attributing prospective juror prejudice to the publicity the riot had received, Judge Pippen noted that Dallas County sentiment "is overwhelmingly against the State's case without regard to the facts or guilt of those engaged in violation of the law" and transferred the hearings to the Travis County District Court.

J.B. McCasland's arson trial commenced in Austin in June of 1931 and he was convicted in a matter of weeks. In July he pled guilty to a charge of rioting and the three other charges against him were dismissed. McCasland was sentenced to two years for each offense, and the sixty-six cases against the other defendants were then transferred to Cooke County (Gainesville).

In Gainesville, County Attorney William C. Culp asked for a dismissal of the indictments against Roy Allen, Jimmie Arnold, C.E. Briggs, Leslie Cole, Jim May, Alvin Morgan, Leonard (Baldy) O'Neal, Horace Reynolds, Bill Sofey and Cleo Wolfe because he believed the evidence against them was insufficient to ensure a conviction. The court agreed and released all ten. Cases against remaining defendants Jeff Jones, Webb Purdom and Jess Roper were scheduled for January 1932.

On June 3, 1932, the indictments against Jones, Purdom and Roper were dismissed (with the consent of the Grayson County district attorney) due to insufficient evidence by Cooke County Judge Ben W. Boyd.

The January 6, 2021 insurrection has its roots in the presidential election of George W. Bush. An uninformed electorate greases the wheels for the status quo. The powers that be prefer us incurious.[25]

Evolve, Please

Fort Worth Weekly March 25, 2009

The best aren't necessarily found at the top of the heap—and vice versa.

On George W. Bush's first day on the job, thousands of folks protested his arguably illegitimate inauguration,[26] and the presidential limo was egged en route to the White House. Last December, as his presidency was coming to a close, an Iraqi reporter named Muntathar al-Zaidi threw his shoes at Bush and yelled, "This is a farewell kiss from the Iraqi people, you dog!"

The most powerful moron in the modern world had come full circle, and we got to watch the entire spectacle from the disenfranchised peanut gallery known as the middle class. The country is polarized, demoralized, embarrassed and bitter, but Bush still has the gall to laud his own hatchet job. "I have a great sense of accomplishment," he said. "I am going home with my head held high."

It makes you wonder what exactly it would take to make him bow his head in shame.

Would he have had to sit by while a major American city was destroyed by a hurricane and then bungle the recovery efforts? What about deceiving millions of American families into sending their loved ones on fools' errands for Big Oil and Bush's cronies in the military-industrial complex? Would he have bowed his head if hundreds of American servicemen and women had been encouraged to torture unarmed prisoners? Would bringing this nation to the brink of financial disaster have been enough?

In my opinion, Bush's greatest accomplishment was an unintended one. He single-handedly demolished all the arguments in favor of the socio-economic theory most beloved by conservatives: Social Darwinism.

For decades, Republicans and conservatives—even though many of them hypocritically reject Darwin's evolutionary theories of human origins—have championed the idea that "survival of the fittest" should be the only rule in the struggle for a decent life. They proclaim that government should not meddle with that human competition by regulating the economy or addressing social problems, and they justify the imbalances and inequality thus created by suggesting that some folks are just better fit to survive and/or excel than others—and everyone else will just have to settle for whatever they get.

When Katrina demolished New Orleans, many conservatives said it was full of lazy welfare cases anyway, and they were just looking for another handout to rebuild government-subsidized housing.

When less financially secure young men and women—who joined the military in part to get help with college—were forced to go and fight our recent wars in Iraq and Afghanistan and had their tours extended or multiplied or were stop-lossed or denied post-traumatic stress discharges, many conservatives simply shrugged their shoulders and said, "Tough luck. Nobody made them sign up."

And when the middle and lower classes began to founder on the rocks of unemployment, meager pay, and the credit crunch, conservatives suggested that it's no accident that these folks occupy the lower rungs of the socio-economic ladder. As conservative talk-radio host Bill Cunningham[27] specifically phrased it, "people are poor in America . . . not because they lack money; they're poor because they lack values, morals, and ethics."

The problem with these rationales and, of course, most justifications of Social Darwinism, is that they recklessly presuppose that this system actually results in quality rising to the top (and inferior folks, by correlation, sinking to the bottom). "Dubya," himself, is the strongest evidence that this is unadulterated poppycock.

That's right, our last president.

You know.

George W. Bush.

The entire Bush administration was a superb model of kakistocracy (i.e., government by the least fit). He didn't ascend to the highest office in the nation by being smarter, wiser, or even more adept at leading people. After coasting along via all the breaks and benefits of familial wealth and political clout, he simply had the right name, the right good ol' boy demeanor, and a little help from a severely compromised electoral system. Instead of natural selection, we got an imbecilic insurrection. Instead of survival of the fittest, we got the rape and pillaging of America for the benefit of those who condoned torture, thievery, ruinous financial policies, and unnecessary war.

Obviously, the dirty little secret behind this pseudo-meritocracy is that the rich and powerful have no intention of maintaining a level playing field. They put their children in the best private schools, get them wartime military deferments, provide them with the best contacts and networking opportunities, and give them a succession of get-out-of-jail-free passes and no-bid contracts.

As the Obama administration attempts to extricate us from the current economic minefield, I hope his staff realizes that our problems aren't just a matter of regulation. We also need to make sure the conservative sham of Social Darwinism goes the way of the dodo.

Half the bozos who complain about folks speaking Spanish in this country can be found listening to conservative talk radio shows while sitting in the drive-thrus of Taco Bell, Taco Bueno, Taco Cabana and Taco Casa every day around lunch time.

Press One for English

Fort Worth Weekly February 19, 2020

Early in the spring semester of my junior year in high school, I had some trouble in Spanish. I hadn't really been paying attention, much less studying, and was too far behind to recover. I found myself relying on crib sheets that were being secretly passed up and down the aisles during every test or quiz. After one particularly important exam, our Spanish instructor noticed that most of the scores and answers were the same.

Cue a long, sideways glance at the biggest juvenile delinquent in the class: me.

Our instructor called me up to her desk, accused me of cheating, and gave me a zero.

It was her prerogative, of course, and she was also right, regardless of my being singled out. But I lost my cool.

Loudly and ill-advisedly, I informed her that the whole *f&#%@ing* class was cheating, and it was *bull$#!t* that I was the fall guy. Our Spanish instructor sent me to the principal's office, where the big guy was so disgusted to see me—did I mention I was something of a frequent flyer—he didn't even ask what I'd done.

I didn't name the originator of said cheat-sheet. In fact, they didn't even ask who it was. Things blew over quickly at school, and my parents were the source of most of the fallout.

Consequently, my mother found a Spanish tutor (one of her friends) posthaste and made me attend Spanish sessions three times a week. I wasn't enthusiastic at first, but her daughter was a cheerleader and joined in on some of the lessons. My interest grew. I became better at Spanish in no time, but, when finals came around, I needed a perfect 100 to pass for the semester.

Cue the drum roll.

I scored a 108 with extra credit points.

More importantly, I picked up a lot of Spanish that was useful for my foreign language requirement in college—where I never cheated—and during numerous trips and vacations over the years around Mexico, Costa Rica, Spain, Peru, Nicaragua, and . . . *Texas*.

Yep.

Texas.

I don't understand the typical anti-immigrant crack, "You're in America! Speak the language!"

We *are* in Texas, and here—*in Texas*—there is a significant percentage of our citizens who don't speak English, especially well. And that's always been the case. That's why foreign languages, particularly Spanish, are part of our school curricula. *Una buena parte.*

The greatest repercussion of Putin's slow, cozy putsch in Russia is Pussy Riot.[28]

Memo To Media Outlets: To Regain Our Trust, Keep it Real (Not Safe)

Dissident Voice May 24th, 2007

Last month, Russian journalists were put on notice. President Vladimir Putin's government informed them that fifty percent of the news they reported had to be positive.

This meant that no matter what was going on in Russian society—plague, pestilence, corruption or another Chernobyl—members of the press corps had to ensure that their reporting informed the Russian public that its cup was at least half full.[29]

A leader like Putin obviously prefers news that portrays the cup running over, but in a Stalin-esque gesture of compromise, he instructed journalists to meet him halfway. Or else.

The good news is, every story may have some good news. The bad news is, bad news may be reported as good news.

If another Chernobyl occurs, Russian journalists will simply have to report that although a nuclear meltdown has poisoned thousands and will lead to ghastly genetic mutations, thousands of acres around the damaged nuclear facility will become dirt-cheap real estate and it'll be a buyer's market. After a stark headline announcing the catastrophe, a subhead will say Invest now, comrade, and the government will throw in a six-legged cow.

It's easy to be smug and poke fun at the hapless Russians, but the truth is we're not a whole lot better off. Our founding fathers made special provisions for a free press in the First Amendment to the U.S. Constitution but, unfortunately, our press isn't really free. Especially to do the job it was meant to do.

Media outlets pay the bills with advertising revenues. These revenues are generated by businesses or large corporations that can afford large advertising budgets. These companies are generally politically conservative and solely devoted to increasing their profit margins. Their top priorities usually preclude forward thinking, social accountability and adherence to methods of long-term, responsible productivity. From this point forward, they become entities media outlets should be criticizing, not receiving their marching orders from.

Profit-mongering sponsors truncate a serious media outlet's most indispensable functions, preventing it from keeping us informed, scrutinizing our political processes and challenging us to stay abreast of the events that define or confine our existence. In short, corporate America obstructs long-term media vigilance to ensure its own short-term economic prosperity.

It works like this: controversial reporting, expository programming and challenging editorial commentary confound, frustrate and unsettle Joe Q. Public. Joe Q. Public tunes out anything he doesn't agree with or like to hear. Corporate advertisers want Joe Q. Public's attention (especially in the form of a receptive predisposition). If a well-meaning media outlet interrupts Joe Q. Public's pleasant daydreams or airs or publishes something large corporate advertisers think might wake Joe Q. Public up or scratch his head or simply grimace, they seek other outlets to peddle their wares.

Most media outlets cannot afford to let this happen, but if they allow corporate America to involve them in profit-mongering or force them to pander to the whims of Joe Q. Public, the free press no longer fulfills its mission. It simply mimics contemporary politicians who follow the path of least resistance and try to please everyone during a campaign year. But unlike an elected representative, a media outlet's campaign runs year-round, year after year.

In the last eight months, the weekday circulation of the average U.S. newspaper has fallen two percent. The weekday circulation of our hometown newspaper, the *Fort Worth Star Telegram*, fell almost four percent.

This drastic drop-off obviously led in some way to the paper's new aesthetic reconfiguration. Staffers redesigned the entire broadsheet, incorporating *USA Today*-like graphics, switching to posh typography and utilizing simpleton-friendly copy arrangements.

But the problem with declining newspaper circulations and discredited media outlets is not the packaging. It's the product. For most of the last seven years, our press has not done its job. Up until the last year or so, it let President Bush and the Republican Party lead it around by the nose, told Joe Q. Public what he wanted to hear (instead of what he needed to hear), and remained blasé and noncommittal when it should have been blistering.

The American media has lost its credibility and new layouts and/or complimentary colors are not going to restore it. Fortunately—for the first time in a long time—Joe Q. Public is weary of political charade, open to dissenting voices and ripe for spirited forums.

Instead of spiffing up the décor, media outlets like the *Star Telegram* need to rededicate themselves to watchful diligence and editorial courage. For instance, the *Telegram* needs to resuscitate or sufficiently replace Molly Ivins (Garrison Keillor is insightful and fun, but too abstract) and jettison asinine, Neocon apologists like Cal Thomas[30] and Don Erler.[31] Thomas and Erler bet on the wrong horse and now all they spend their copy space doing is qualifying their original, unenlightened positions.

The *Telegram* doesn't have to take a side; it just needs to stop hedging its bets. The Bush devolution is over and media obsequiousness is no longer a sound business plan.

Skip the nifty graphics and bring on fresh voices, singular vision and editorial integrity. Something like *Fox News*, except with heart and a conscience.

The cup was more than half empty in this country for a long time. Give it to us genuinely and straight and your ratings and readership will climb.

And this was a decade ago. These days the Red numbskulls don't even bother with legitimate rationales or justifications.

"Actionable" Unintelligence: They'll Have to Pry Our Ignorance from Our Cold Dumb Credos

Dissident Voice January 13th, 2010

In the recent writings and discussions I've perused regarding Umar Farouk Abdulmutallab's attempted terrorist attack on Northwest Airlines Flight 253, I've heard a lot of talk about "actionable" intelligence. Did the Obama administration have "actionable" intelligence regarding Abdulmutallab? Did the CIA, FBI or Homeland Security have "actionable" intelligence and, if they did, why didn't they connect the dots and take action? These are legitimate questions, but not ones that we as a people or culture like to answer.

The *Fox News* loop was quick to blame our young president for almost not keeping us safe. Some members of the G.O.P. intelligentsia even went as far as saying that nothing like this ever happened under the Bush Administration because Bush kept us safe.

"Kept us safe" is a popular Neocon talking point but, of course, it's a bald-face lie. 9/11 occurred on President Bush's watch and it's an established fact that his administration had "actionable" intelligence pointing to a possible 9/11-type strike, but didn't act. Especially in any way that might have averted the attack.

It's also fairly established that we didn't have serious, "actionable" intelligence regarding Weapons of Mass Destruction (WMDs) in Iraq. But, in that case, we did act.

I'm not writing here to rub anybody's face in it. I just think the American people deserve a little honesty. They also deserve some blame.

We are surrounded by "actionable" intelligence every day. We just don't do anything about it. It's too complicated or inconvenient. It might require us to think for ourselves. It's easier to just parrot the pundits that reinforce views we're already comfortable with.

For example, it's abundantly clear that our healthcare system is on pace to bankrupt us. But one political party and the powers behind it are bent on blocking reform and fomenting doubt about the problem. It's easier to tune in to Rush Limbaugh and hear the "actionable" intelligence undermined than have to act on it.

For another example, it's abundantly clear that human beings are having a detrimental effect on the planet and their own ecosystem. But one political party and the powers behind it are bent on blocking environmental legislation and—you guessed it—fomenting doubts about the problem. It's easier to turn the channel to *Fox News* and, again, watch the "actionable" intelligence be undermined rather than have to act on it.

There is clearly an abundance of good, "actionable" intelligence out there, but acting on it is simply not our strong suit. We see it or hear it and simply ignore it. It interferes with our plans. It complicates our goals and values. It makes going along to get along wrong and immoral–but going along to get along is how we get by in this world. It's how we pay the bills and keep a roof over our heads. It's tried and true, and besides, the path of least resistance is paved with glory and gold.

Where would the world be if the Bush Administration had acted on "actionable" intelligence and foiled 9/11? Without a fierce new fire and brimstone adversary to replace the Soviet Union, the American military-industrial complex would probably be in its final death throes. America would still have been a dwindling superpower, but at least with troops on the ground in Iraq and Afghanistan we could remain the most dangerous country on the planet. And with our domestic industries being shipped overseas and the middle-class dead or dying, at least we still have war to make. And sell.

Blackwater (now called Xe) now retains the world's largest stable of mercenary killers, and they'll deliver or dispose of the goods above or beyond the law. Halliburton (aka *Warmart*) is now the planet's most profitable big box carnage shop and, if you've got a populace to pacify or foes to eliminate, they'll provide the infrastructure and guns *. . . and for a limited time only, they'll throw the body bags in for FREE!*

The world isn't any safer, but the danger gives us an excuse for keeping our war machine revved up and stoking our brawn and bluster.

Without the War on Terror we surely would have faced a great depression. Or an identity crisis. Maybe even a psychotic break.

All we have to do now is find a way to keep the War on Terror going . . . at least until we can come up with another enemy. And then we don't have to change anything.

The Stars and Stripes brand may lose its market value and eventually wind up in the dustbin of empires, but at least we'll fade with our boots on and our depravity intact.

A little dated now that Get Out, *etc., have been released, but still worth a read. Constance Hollie-Jawaid and I both spoke and were each presented American flags that had flown over the Houses of Congress in Washington, D. C. The honorary* Stars and Stripes *were provided by Texas Senator John Cornyn (who was not in attendance), and I think I frustrated my hosts when I remarked under my breath that Cornyn was practically a Nazi. It was still a great event.*

The Struggle Is Real

A speech I gave for Black Citizens for Justice, Law and Order, a group of racial justice advocates in Dallas. September 24, 2016

When I was originally approached by Daisy Joe[32] about speaking here today, she let me know that the main theme was: The struggle is real.

The struggle is real. And, obviously, on many fronts—it's still not being won. We've got a tremendous amount of work to do. It's not something I simply believe. It's something I see with my own eyes.

After I agreed to participate in this important event, I decided to edit a collection of Texas horror stories. Texas horror by Texas authors. My last two books, *The 1910 Slocum Massacre: An Act of Genocide in East Texas* and *Black Holocaust: The Paris Horror and a Legacy of Texas Terror*, had both chronicled loathsome chapters in Texas history—and black history. I thought editing a collection of fictional horror stories would be a nice break from the disturbing nonfiction material I'd spent the last few years researching. I was looking forward to it. But my respite was short-lived.

From the outset, I worked to get stories from a diverse field of horror writers. I quickly found, however, that the field wasn't terribly diverse. Few persons of color, and particularly black folks, wrote horror in Texas. It surprised me. But it wasn't just Texas. Few black folks wrote horror at all.

The horror genre in books and movies is primarily the purview of white authors and white audiences. And, as informed as I liked to think I am, this had never occurred to me before. And the obvious question I asked myself was, why?

Eddie Murphy used to puzzle over why white people would stay in haunted houses in the movies. I remember in *Delirious*, a comedy concert from 1983, he cracked jokes about white folks staying in the house featured in *The Amityville Horror* even after their toilet filled with blood and the house explicitly told them to leave. He said white people simply say stuff like, "Hmmm. That's peculiar" and stay. While he in the same position would have said, "I love this house, baby, but we got to get the [expletive] out."

It's a great bit and, though Murphy didn't explore it too deeply, it makes an important point. I doubt the supposition that black people would leave a house after it told them to leave explains why there are very few black horror writers. Actually, I think the fact that crazy white folks would stay gets closer to the real story behind the issue. You see, white folks watch horror movies for titillation, suspense and excitement. They like being scared. It allows them to flirt with danger or terror without really having to experience it.

That's the truth. Most folks that look and walk and talk like me, don't have much experience with real danger. Or real horror. So we go to the movies to experience it vicariously.

Think about the top horror films you watched over the years. What was the subject matter? What did they deal with?

Exorcist. A white daughter is possessed by a demon.

The Shining. A white family in an old hotel for white people is attacked by ghosts.

Halloween. A white babysitter for a white family in a white neighborhood gets attacked by a psychopath.

Friday the 13th. A bunch of horny white counselors at a summer camp for white kids are slaughtered.

Nightmare on Elm Street. More dumb white kids are slaughtered.

76

Texas Chainsaw Massacre. Dumb white teenagers get made into BBQ.

Poltergeist. White suburbia is attacked.

The Omen. Atticus Finch gets attacked by the devil's white baby. (The only really good horror movie featuring a black man as the protagonist—that I can remember in recent years—is *Fallen*, with Denzel Washington. Good black cop attacked by demon.)

Books and films in the horror genre almost never feature anyone other than white protagonists. And those inexpressible, horrifying monsters hiding in white people's spacious middle-class closets or under their memory foam beds are almost always some obscure, fictional witch or demon or devil or ghost. It's scary to us—but it's also fun. We white folks live lives of relative security and ease. And the truth is, there's very little real horror in white lives these days, or even in the last century or so—unless we experienced it personally in a war or a natural disaster. Real live horror is mostly foreign to us. So we invent it. And we are entertained by it.

Now, I'm obviously white. I forget that sometimes on a dance floor or a basketball court. But my beautiful, mixed wife patiently reminds me.

I look out over this audience, this gathering, and I see a lot of faces that don't look like mine. And over the last few years I've become a lot more familiar with your history.

And what I've learned, perhaps more than anything else—the thing that so many people who look like me don't seem to understand—is that you're not unfamiliar with horror. Or terror. Or real live monsters.

You don't have to write fictional stories about evil spirits or psychopaths or vengeful creatures to be afraid of or terrified by. You've been surrounded by them for decades. And your struggles against them have been real—not make-believe in a book or on a movie screen.

I can't look back over my personal bloodline and see an ancestor that was transported here against his or her will in chains, in a stinking, disease-ridden ship's keep. Beaten, tortured and starved. A horror of horrors. But I bet some of you can.

I can't look back over my white bloodline and see where members of my family were ever blamed for something they didn't do, and subsequently had their lives taken or their houses blown up, just because of the color of their skin. I bet some of you can.

I can't look back over my white bloodline and see anyone I was related to or anyone who even looked like me who was tortured in public, castrated, stabbed or blinded and then burned at the stake in front of a crowd of thousands of cheering faces, just because of the color of their skin. And I definitely can't look back over my bloodline and find an instance of somebody dressing up in sheets and burning a cross in our front yards. I know some of you can.

Black people don't have to imagine horrific scenarios. Or conjure up terrifying situations or hellish conditions. You don't have to invent creatures or monsters that go bump in the night or try to steal your souls.

They're all around you and they've been around you ever since your ancestors were first brought here against their will. The real monster of black folks' nightmares in America over the last 300 years is not an imaginary creature. It's a living breathing white man.

That ghost out in the woods that looked like a white sheet and floated? That was some guy who probably looked a lot like me on a black horse riding to your grandparents or great-grandparents house to terrorize them or take what was theirs and force them to give up everything they had run for their lives.

That creature outside your door making your parents or your grandparents dread even getting out of bed some days, fearful of what they might be accused of if it was convenient, or what might happen to them if they walked on the wrong side of the sidewalk? That was a white man or a white woman.

And that monster hiding under your bed—he was a white man who raped your daughter or sister or mother. And got away with it. Because white men raping black women (and girls) wasn't even against the law in the old days, and black victims had no recourse.

The struggle was real, then. And it's real now. And so is the horror and the terror.

Heaven forbid your car breaks down in Oklahoma. Heaven forbid you sit in the wrong church in South Carolina. Or your baby boy is playing with a fake gun in the park. Or your daughter knocks on the wrong door for help when her car breaks down. Or your teenage son cuts through the wrong neighborhood with Skittles and a Dr. Pepper. Or your family is too prosperous in the wrong part of Texas.

That's a black horror story that concerns Daisy Joe and Constance Hollie-Jawaid. Some jealous white folks decided they didn't like how successful the black community near Slocum, Texas was, and, on July 29, 1910, they began killing black folks as fast as they could. Mobs of dozens and hundreds of white folks—monsters—started shooting black people down in cold blood, most of them in the back, as many as they could find, cutting telephone lines so they couldn't call out for help, killing men, women and children. And dumping their bodies in mass graves. The Texas Rangers came but by the time they got there, many of the bodies were gone, buried. The black survivors fled for their lives, leaving their homes and properties behind. It was a land grab made possible by a racial expulsion which was sparked by an act of genocide. And hardly anybody had even heard of it a few years back. Now it's known about across the country. Miss Hollie-Jawaid can tell you how real the struggle we fought to see this atrocity remembered and officially memorialized was, I assure you.

A giant oil boom occurred in East Texas not long after Miss Hollie-Jawaid's and Daisy Joe's ancestors lost the hundreds of acres of land they owned in the Slocum area. Hell, there's still oil and gas drilling going on in the area now. *Damn*—that was a close one. The racist white element around Slocum may have saved the United States oil and gas industry from having to deal with an African American oil baron.

But the possible fortune in natural resources that was lost is hardly the scariest part of the story. The scariest part of the story is that most of the bodies of the innocent, unarmed black victims who were slain are still piled up in mass graves out there. We can't get permission to conduct a proper search. And the horror the victims of the Slocum Massacre experienced is compounded by the ongoing travesty that all of them still lay there in unmarked, largely anonymous repose. The struggle is real. And it's not finished.

And one last scary thing.

All the work that Constance Hollie-Jawaid and I did to bring attention to the Slocum Massacre—it was no small accomplishment. But do you know how many major African American publications, channels, broadcast and/or news outlets actually picked up this incredibly compelling piece of forgotten black history and ran with it or, for that matter, even ran a story on it?

One.

The *Atlanta Black Star*.

News One's Roland Martin (who's from Texas) hasn't discussed it. Joy-Ann Reed from *MSNBC* hasn't mentioned it.

And obviously Oprah hasn't contacted Miss Hollie-Jawaid about doing something on it.

We all know why white media outlets might avoid this subject matter. But why are black media outlets ignoring it? Oh yeah, the struggle is real. And not just with white monsters—but with black complacence and apathy. We need everybody for this struggle. We need all hands on deck to get this history told. The Tulsa Race Massacre and the Rosewood Massacre have gotten prime time attention. The Slocum Massacre is neglected and ignored in comparison.

Is the struggle real? Definitely. We're waging it every day.

Are there two separate Americas, one white, one black? Hell, yes. And only one group really has to walk around in constant fear. The other group is ignorant to this reality and simultaneously responsible for it.

The struggle is real because the horror is real. Not all white people are part of the problem any more than all black people are part of the solution. But there aren't enough black or white people like Constance Hollie-Jawaid, Daisy Joe, the Black Citizens for Justice, Law and Order, or the Hollie family in general taking this struggle seriously.

I admit it. Sometimes I count my chickens before they hatch. Wendy Davis was no match for "Captain Texas," and Hillary Clinton lost to Donald J. Trump. The preposterous farce that followed was obviously well-nigh insufferable, but I thought this satirical was spot on.

Blunder Games
Unpublished July 14, 2013

There's a lot of dumb in the heart of Texas these days. And a lot of evil.

On the bright side the Governor of Dumb [Rick Perry] won't be sticking around to debate the smart, boycotting woman from Fort Worth in the 2014 governor's race. But Governor Dumb probably will sign a new anti-abortion law that treats ladies and cowgirls like they're incompetent and can't be trusted with the final say regarding what should or should not be permitted regarding their own bodies, persons and/or reproductive judgments.

It's an insulting dystopian vision. The working title is "Blunder Games." The plot is almost Margaret Atwood-esque,[33] except no brains, less conscience and very little verisimilitude. In a time in the very near future, women are weak-willed, unaccountable twists that allow blameless fecundators to impregnate them and then dare to terminate the fruits of their irresponsibility. They're cast out, shunned or, even better, made to endure invasive vaginal procedures or watch fetal porn. The wise, white, patriarchal elders look on at the tribulations of the women approvingly. Pills and elixirs have made the pasty elders once again potent and the destruction of their seed must be outlawed. Non-white, non-elders and less-white alien invaders are reproducing like a plague and the male, recently re-potent wise elders must prevent white, less pasty, non-elder females from reducing the white population. It stars Jennifer Lawrence before she made it big (because her first agent sucked) and Jason Robards,[34] who had been dead for years before production even started, but who—even as a corpse—so cannily nailed the part of the leader of the wise, white, patriarchal elders during auditions that the director, Ridley Scott,[35] had to have him.

In the end, Lawrence's character, "Incubator 931," aborts Robards' character's unwanted, pasty, omega fetus with a laser ladle and bleeds to death, but blows up the entire Chamber of Elders (looking strangely like the state capitol building of Texas) where the male, recently re-potent wise elders had composed and implemented their nefarious dictums.

This new vision is coming to limited theatres soon but, in the meantime, the Texas GOP (who Robards and Scott claimed they studied for authenticity and phallic posturing before the shoot) are providing a real-time first-look. Under white, pasty, patriarchal, conservative rule, the formal onus (no Republicans, not anus . . . *onus*) for unwanted pregnancies is placed solely on the shoulders of girls and women. Though the fecundating involves a human male and female, the coital male is entirely absolved. The unwanted pregnancy—consensual, non-consensual, un-sensual (i.e., unwitting passed-out coed at a frat party thrown by future white, pasty, patriarchal, conservative), etc.—is strictly chalked-up by the pasty white Republican majority in the Texas legislature as the coital female's weakness or mistake. The assumption is they did this to themselves, and that's why the fecundators face no legal consequences, mandates or restrictions.

Essentially, white, pasty, patriarchal, conservative Republicans in Texas (and across America) are saying "How dare women try to extinguish the frivolous fruit of patriarchal privilege. If you don't

82

support the fetus you don't support the troops, and if women don't like it they should have been born with penises."

Ann Richards and Molly Ivins[36] are laughing in a place that has less and less Republicans and no sausage preachers. And that smart, white, less-pasty, non-patriarchal female state legislator from Fort Worth is licking her chomps. She'll gracefully dunk on whomever the pasty white Lone Star Republican patriarchy nominates to run against her in 2014, well before Hillary Clinton skyhooks over whomever the pasty white national Republican patriarchy nominates in 2016. Their sausage factory act is tired, their re-potence is lame and the *dictums* of their leadership are, well, inadequate and unwanted.

The pasty white club that stands up for the chauvinist side of things spends two-thirds of its normal day complaining about the polarization that cripples the nation and the other one-third devising and passing unpopular legislation that challenges longstanding, established rights that most of America takes for granted. Meanwhile, back at Niggerhead Ranch,[37] call girls and hooded teenagers with Skittles are still aborted by itchy, desperate conservatives with guns and most of us look on in frustrated disbelief.

Don't fret, dear protagonists. The worm is turning and the GOP is squirming. They took their "Blunder Games" to asininity and beyond, but the credits on their dystopian vision will be running soon.

"Dear future generations: Please accept our apologies. We were rolling drunk on petroleum."
— Kurt Vonnegut

So It Goes

Fort Worth Weekly July 8, 2020

More than 130,000 Americans dead from a global pandemic.

So it goes.

A cretinous, incorrigible *jagaloon* slinging excrement from the Oval Office.

So it goes.

A nation once straining toward greatness, now on the verge of collapse (due to its own greed and shortsightedness).

So it goes.

A species—ours—pushing its own habitat to the edge of ecological and environmental disaster.

So it's going.

Kurt Vonnegut has been dead for thirteen years, but he's not done with us yet. I'm not real sure he ever will be. And I keep thinking back to a first chapter exchange in *Slaughterhouse Five*.

A character based on Vonnegut tells a filmmaker that the book he has written is an antiwar novel, and the filmmaker mocks him. "Why don't you write an anti-glacier book instead?" the filmmaker says.

The implication, of course, is that wars are as inevitable as glaciers. Which seemed clever in 1969, the year *Slaughterhouse Five* was released. Maybe even edgy. Glaciers were still a constant in 1969.

But things have changed.

Today, wars go on endlessly, and glaciers disappear. Today, the oceans warm, acidify, and rise, and the American military-industrial complex sinks to all new lows. And the United States, once looked upon as a beacon of light, is increasingly viewed as a harbinger of darkness.

The American response to the COVID-19 pandemic hasn't given anyone who's been paying attention much hope that things are going to get better, but they have to. We must make sure of it for ours and our neighbors' sakes, for our species' sake, and all the other species' sakes. Self-destruction is not Holy Writ. We're on the precipice of what comes next—and the last next, if we're not careful.

When so many things can no longer go on, the irony of Vonnegut's "So it goes" is as biting and incisive as ever and as deadly as, dare I say, war. Because it's become a war for those who embrace consciousness. A war for sustainability and survival.

For the latter half of the last century, Vonnegut's "So it goes" was a taunt to consider and weigh for anybody with a conscience. Today, it's a dire challenge that demands rebuke from everyone who remains sentient. "So it goes" is no longer an acceptable quip. Things can no longer go on as they have. The old rules and the old rulers must be cast aside.

The horrors Vonnegut witnessed during the firebombing of Dresden are tame compared to what the future may hold for us. We're on a path toward extinction, not distinction.

Almost ten years to the day before Republican nut-jobs mounted an insurrection at the U.S. Capitol Building on January 6, 2021, a Conservative gun nut opened fire on a crowd outside a Safeway grocery store in Casas Adobes, Arizona (a suburban area northwest of Tucson), with a 9mm pistol with a 33-round magazine. He hit nineteen people, killing six, among them U.S. House of Representative Gabrielle Giffords, federal judge John Roll and a 9-year-old child, Christina-Taylor Green. And "Captain Texas" just signed a bill allowing Republican nut-jobs and gun nuts to open carry without licensing or regulation.

Republicans and Their Guns
Dissident Voice January 12, 2011

Republicans can disavow responsibility for Jared Loughner all they want, but he was wearing Christine O'Donnell's[38] "man-pants," he did exercise Sharron Angle's[39] interpretation of the 2nd Amendment, and he did use conservative radio host Joyce Kaufman's bullets when the ballots didn't work. Oh, and he did get a Democrat in Sarah Palin's[40] bull's eye crosshairs.

Most folks are tiptoeing around the partisan nature of the shooting of U.S. Congresswoman Gabrielle Giffords and others in Tucson, but count me among the uncouth. There is blood on conservative hands and they should be called out. Another homicidal nut-job has brought their irresponsible rhetoric to fruition and they should answer for it.

I don't want to hear Republicans saying there's no place for this kind of violence in this country or condemning Loughner as an isolated, incidental mad man. Especially as if it's something new or unexpected. Conservative rhetoric has been cranked up way past the "stun" setting ever since the Bush Administration was on its last crooked leg. And the target audience for their hate-speak has clearly been compelled.

Lest we forget, it was a conservative who walked into his former church in Knoxville, Tennessee on July 28, 2008 and shot eight people (killing two) because liberals "were ruining the country" (and his church had gotten too liberal). It was conservatives who were brandishing firearms at political events in the 2008 presidential campaign. It was a conservative evangelical Christian who shot abortion doctor George Tiller[41] at his church in Kansas on May 31, 2009. It was a conservative white supremacist who shot security guard Stephen Tyrone Johns[42] at the Holocaust Museum on June 10, 2009. And it was arguably an anti-government conservative that flew his plane into the IRS office in Austin, Texas on February 10, 2010.

There is no reason to mince words.

Violence is implicit in conservative rhetoric because its audience honestly believes dissenters should be vilified and punished, and it thrills the Republicans' conservative base to see its philosophical opponents squirm. Threatening language is necessary for their cause because fear and hatred are presently the load-bearing joists in their political platform. And what's more, deep down, they're not even ashamed of it.

Rush Limbaugh once blamed John Edwards' affair with Rielle Hunter on Elizabeth Edwards, now deceased. He said that John Edwards[43] sought companionship with Hunter because, unlike his wife, Rielle "did something with her mouth other than talk." It was callous and repugnant, but it wasn't scripted, and it didn't diminish Limbaugh's ratings one iota. The comment was telling about who Limbaugh is and how he thinks, but also about who his audience is and how they think. The truth is, it's not hard to imagine Limbaugh serving up something equally asinine about Congresswoman Giffords. Right now, he wouldn't dare because there's too much heat. But just because he isn't saying it doesn't mean he's not thinking it.

And this is why Limbaugh is the voice for so many conservatives in this country. He touches a nerve with his listeners; he teases a brutish, authoritarian strain in them that reveres clichés like "my country right or wrong," "love it or leave it," etc. And these folks take comfort in implied threats for people who disagree with them. That's why they can rationalize the notion that the ends justify the means.

Deep down, they're not really bothered by the combustible letter that was sent to Janet Napolitano;[44] she's from the wrong side of the aisle. And somewhere inside they're not terribly upset by what happened to Giffords, because she's the ideological enemy. They can't help themselves. It's just who they are.

But one of these days a sharp contrarian will finally expose it. It will be like that showdown scene from *A Few Good Men*. The contrarian will get a Limbaugh or a Beck or a Palin or an Allen West on a "stand" and challenge their methods and their authority and their warped world view and badger them and demand the truth; and then that Limbaugh, Beck, Palin or West will say the rest of us can't handle the truth and launch into a blustery diatribe explaining that heathens like Tiller and liberals like Giffords got what they had coming to them, and the country is a better place with every less one of them around.

And everyone will be shocked and offended except those in gun-toting red states who, deep down, can see what Limbaugh, Beck, Palin and West were really trying to say, before they were misquoted or misinterpreted.

When George W. Bush ran against Governor Ann Richards for the reins of Texas in 1991, he actually mistook the state bird of Texas—a Mockingbird—for a dove, and shot it at a staged hunting event. Bush still got elected. This omen obviously portended what his governorship and presidency would be like.

The Real Ground Zero

Fort Worth Weekly July 5, 2006

On February 9, 2001, two American civilians (no doubt big George Bush presidential campaign contributors) were permitted to take the *USS Greenville* (a 7,000-ton nuclear submarine) for a joyride in the middle of the Pacific Ocean.

They scooted around a bit underwater and then dramatically (i.e., hastily) surfaced. Unfortunately, the *Ehime Maru*, a Japanese fishing research vessel, was sitting directly above. It sank rapidly. Nine people died, and four were high school students.

President Bush immediately tasked Colin Powell to send the president's apologies and condolences to the Japanese prime minister; but the American civilians at the helm of the submarine were never identified.

Eight months later, Islamic extremists flew domestic passenger airplanes into the World Trade Center and the Pentagon.

What Bush (and we) didn't know then was that 9/11 was the historic windfall of his presidency. Until then, he had earned very little respect and even less clout. But 9/11 dropped into his lap, and the country did what it always does when it's attacked or threatened. We rallied around the flag.

It's ludicrous to say Bush rose to the occasion. A public still divided by his ascendance to the presidency (via the U.S. Supreme Court) became a united constituency in response to a shared enemy. Supporters and detractors fell in line.

For a while, Bush flourished as a "wartime" president, and he could do no wrong. But he and the diabolical brain trust that preps him and props him up in front of the teleprompters got greedy.

Forgetting Bush's clumsiness before 9/11, they were emboldened to start a war with a country that had nothing to do with the attack. With the American public still in synchronized patriot mode, the Bush brain trust insidiously circulated unsubstantiated reports of WMDs in Iraq and then vociferously proclaimed ties between Osama Bin Laden[45] and Iraq and Al Qaeda and Saddam Hussein. Before the public could take a breath, we invaded Iraq.

Billed as little more than a Boy Scout retreat, Operation Iraqi Freedom saw the U.S. Military quickly drop a bunch of bombs and send Saddam into hiding. But after the special effects ended and the Iraqis realized Kilroy[46] wasn't leaving anytime soon, they grew weary of patting us on the back. Iraq's political, economic, and utility systems were demolished, and we had no real formulated plans to rebuild the infrastructure.

Fundamentalist Muslims began calling our presence in Iraq an affront to Islam. Volunteers began lining up all over the Middle East for their shot at seventy-two virgins. The invasion became a nation-building occupation, which created a contrary Islamic insurgency where there was none before.

Meanwhile, back at home, the war was dragging on and another presidential election was coming up, so the brain trust began issuing terror alerts any time Dubya had a dip in the polls. And while they were on a roll, they decided to start new wars—on homosexuality and abortion. It had worked before. No one remembered the *Ehime Maru* and the clumsy early months of the Bush presidency. They just remembered George W. parading around on an aircraft carrier. Folks who questioned the war were "flip-floppers," and anyone who disagreed with the Republican Party's Christian Fundamentalist leanings was immoral, if not un-American.

President Bush was re-elected, and the Republican Party proceeded with business as usual. But the American public had begun to recover from its lapse into unreasoning synchronicity. And the ridiculously villainous antics of George's first term began to haunt the administration. The outing of CIA agent Valerie Plame left egg on their face, and Vice President Cheney without his top aide. The Bush Administration's fingerprints were all over Abu Ghraib. Republican interference in the Terry Schiavo case[47] backfired. Republican attempts to strip the lower and middle classes of Social Security exploded on the launch pad.

Texan Michael Brown,[48] another civilian improperly placed at the helm of a federal vehicle, whiffed on Hurricane Katrina.[49] Gasoline shot up to $3 a gallon while Bush's extended family in the oil business piled up obscene profits. Bush's attempt to put a United Arab Emirates conglomerate in charge of American port security was scoffed at roundly. And the Republican party's rejection of evolution and global warming began to be recognized as backward, ignorant, and irresponsible.

The Bush charade is finally unraveling, but for too many of us, "Ground Zero" is now the country where we live.

The American public's faith in its political leaders is the lowest it's been since Watergate (where Cheney and Donald Rumsfeld learned the tools of the trade). Our beleaguered troops are still in Iraq. Progress in religious tolerance, race relations, and lifestyle freedoms has been set back forty years. The budget surpluses of the 1990s have been replaced by a trade deficit that approaches infinity.

The Bush administration's handling of the *Ehime Maru* incident was the rule, not the exception. And, if not for 9/11, it would have endured as a forecast of his presidential tenure.

It's hard to be heartened in the rubble, but we have to look forward. Midterm elections are just around the corner.

Lambasting your hometown is hardly wise, but Aledo—like the rest of the state—gets too many things wrong to deserve a break.

Life's Too Short to Live in Aledo
May 6, 2011

If you dine or drink at the local Railhead BBQ on Montgomery Street in Fort Worth, it's hard not to notice the slogan on the waitstaff's t-shirts. It says "Life's too short to live in Dallas."

The sentiment exploits our natural distaste for Big D and plays on what's probably the biggest civic rivalry in Texas. It's a successful marketing ploy for Railhead, but their attempt to replicate it at their second location in Aledo flounders. The Railhead t-shirts in Aledo say "Life's too short to live in Southlake."

I grew up in Aledo and don't remember having any serious beefs with Southlake, but there are two points of contention between the communities that Railhead successfully stokes. The first is big money suburbia. Aledo is obviously no longer a farm town.

Aledo real estate is astronomical and affluent, child-raising guppies (graying urban professionals) have descended upon the community like locusts, attracted to its diminishing small-town feel, limited lower class demographics and socio-economic restricted ethnic diversity. Aledo and Southlake have some of these qualities in

92

common and obviously compete for the West-o-plex's white bread, snobby dollar.

The second point of contention is big-time high school football. Of late, Aledo has supplanted Southlake as the well-to-do West-o-plex community bringing home the state championship bacon, attracting local talent, producing top recruits and making its mark in the annals of Texas high school football season after season.

In terms of prosperous suburbanites and gridiron supremacy, Southlake and Aledo both resemble one another and compete, but there's one, giant, incontrovertible difference, and it concerns how they received the natural gas industry.

When the Barnett Shale-baggers rolled into this part of Texas to tap our natural gas deposits, Aledo rolled out the red carpet and yelled, "Frack Baby, Frack." No one worried about air pollution. No one wondered what would happen to local water sources. Nobody asked questions about the long-term repercussions of fracking, injecting spent drilling pollutants into disposal wells or dumping them in evaporation pits. The Shale-baggers had Aledo at "Howdy, sign here."

For the last several years, the presence of drilling toxins and "fracking" compounds have steadily increased in our water and air supplies, but we've been repeatedly assured that they comprise "trace" amounts or are still well below hazardous thresholds. In other words, the trace amounts are hazardous, but not in the short-term. And no one knows what the long-term effects will be, so don't worry, be happy. Or at least be compensated for the imposition.

The issue begged serious scrutiny, but it never came. Sure, it was nice for a lot of folks who made a quick buck or kept a steady-paying gig through this stretching recession—but should it have been done at the expense of the long-term health of the community?

Southlake received the Shale-baggers a little differently.

When XTO and friends stepped into Southlake, they didn't expect to find a bunch of greedy, hickish dupes like the folks they fleeced in Bearcat Country, but they certainly didn't anticipate what they got: a bunch of concerned, informed, forward-thinking citizens who were more interested in clean air than being taken to the cleaners.

Southlakers protested. Southlakers filed a lawsuit. The Shale-baggers were confronted with yard signs that said "Get the frack out of here" and "Don't frack with me."

The Shale-baggers—who were used to getting their way, especially after the way Aledo (and Fort Worth) licked their boots—were taken aback and bailed, dropping their plans to drill at the only site Southlake had approved.

Now don't get me wrong. I'm no fan of Southlake. But at least the folks in Dragon Land weren't a doormat for the natural gas industry. And at least the snobs up there have an environmental IQ.

Life may be too short to live in Southlake, but it's also too short to live anywhere that folks are too greedy for their own good.

Check that. I forgot.

We live in America.

God botherers bother me, partie deux.

In Gaffes We Trust
Fort Worth Weekly May 9, 2018

Every time I see a Tarrant County tax statement—specifically of the variety I have to pay—it irritates me, but probably not for the reasons you think.

I don't mind paying taxes, and I don't even feel I'm overtaxed. I simply believe our political representatives spend too much of our tax money on what they shouldn't and not enough on what they should. I also know they give obscene tax breaks to persons and corporate personhoods that they absolutely should not.

Beyond that, I'm not comfortable with Jesus' lame hedge-your-bet "Render to Caesar the things that are Caesar's; and to God the things that are God's" (Matthew 22:21) or Paul's ludicrous "Let every person be in subjection to the governing authorities . . . for there is no authority except from God and those which exist are established by God" (Romans 13:1).

Was the Third Reich established by God? The Khmer Rouge?
What about Donald Trump?
These issues concern me, but they are not my chief complaint.

What bothers me is the beat-down I experience every time I receive my tax statement and the day I go to pay my tax bill. It's four words printed in neutral gray in the center of the document, just above the perforated tear-line of payment coupon. In larger text than anything else on the page, my Tarrant County tax statement proclaims (in all caps), "IN GOD WE TRUST."

Now, to be perfectly clear, I can understand Tarrant County trying to be right with that old white-haired, therapeutic deity in the sky—especially when so many of its gun-toting citizens court if not outright invite Armageddon. It's Grand Ol' Politics and it plays well to the Christian meek.

But what if my personal spiritual affectations favor chubby Buddha or grouchy Zeus? Tarrant County would clearly marginalize my therapeutic deity, and that's not exactly considerate, decent, or fair. Every tax statement would remind me I was different—an Other—and that the institutions that push this alienating proclamation would be enjoying free, privileged advertising, which is somewhat ludicrous, because, of course, "houses" of God don't even pay taxes.

How would you feel if your Tarrant County tax statement threw in an, "IN VISHNU WE TRUST"? Or (clutches pearls), "IN ALLAH WE TRUST"?

For those of us who are not down with the Bible, "IN GOD WE TRUST" is a subtle taunt. It may be a small thing, but a good community fosters tolerance. And a great community encourages inclusiveness. A majority-pandering proclamation like "IN GOD WE TRUST" diminishes Tarrant County and Fort Worth and makes us less good and not great. In fact, it makes us look ignorant, exclusivist, and narrow-minded.

What is my religion?

It's none of your business, and it doesn't matter. And the same is true of yours and the majority of Tarrant County's.

In one specific God or supreme being *WE DO NOT ALL TRUST.* Not mine, not yours, and certainly not the Tarrant County Tax Assessor-Collector's. And that's a good thing.

Many of our next-door neighbors and national leaders may forget or like to ignore the fact that our revolutionary ideals about the separation of church and state define our national identity and make us great. In fact, these same inconvenient ideals constitute one of the only ways in which we are still truly great.

I realize our coins and paper currency feature "IN GOD WE TRUST," but that's a federal issue. More forward-thinking sorts would have at least used something honest and useful from the Bible—maybe a product warning—like 1 Timothy 6:10, which clearly states, "For the love of money is the root of all evil." But the sycophants who set the presses for "IN GOD WE TRUST" at our mints had to pander to capitalist overlords.

When I go to pay my tax bill, I have to endure a presumptuous, exclusivist, religious proclamation in the body of the tax statement, and then on the back of the payment envelope, the proclamation appears—again. So, after I lick the seal and close the envelope, I'm taunted and alienated once more for good measure. Sort of a "Take that with you, blasphemer, heretic, loser."

The good news is, I take it better than a lot of you would if the roles were reversed. The bad news is, Fort Worth is appealing to a lower, instead of a higher, power.

Bullshit wars require duped citizenries and medicated troops. Unfortunately, every American war starting with (and since) Vietnam, has been bullshit.

Fighting for Sanity

Fort Worth Weekly September 9, 2009

In the last few years the number of suicides involving active-duty American troops has skyrocketed. In addition to engaging the enemy, a growing number of our soldiers are also fighting themselves. And they're losing.

The Army's new solution is "resiliency" training. Instead of completely eliminating the back-door draft or reasonably limiting the number of deployments soldiers and their families have to undergo, Uncle Sam is simply trying to make sure our warriors can better stomach the strains and inequities we have required them to endure.

The logic seems to be that there is nothing wrong with what we're asking them to do; they're simply ill-equipped for the task. According to the *New York Times*, the "resiliency" program will be offered in weekly 90-minute sessions designed "to defuse or expose common habits of thinking and flawed beliefs that can lead to anger and frustration."

Wow.

Here's another theory: Perhaps the "flawed beliefs" that lead our soldiers to thoughts of anger and frustration and perhaps to rage and self-contempt, don't originate in the soldiers so much as in those who have led us into ill-considered, preposterous shams of serious conflicts. If your fellow platoon members die fighting or acting as occupiers or simply in delivering materials to a no-bid, over-budget Halliburton[50] project, you'd like to believe they died for something noble or important or at least understandable. But in our current wars, that belief is hard for many soldiers to maintain. Our troops are caught up in spuriously concocted pre-emptive wars that are so laced with lies and propaganda that in the end they almost appear to be the very thing our men and women in uniform should be fighting against.

Our soldiers can't sincerely claim they're defending our country. And if they shipped out with the old "my-country-right-or-wrong" mentality, many have learned how spirit-crushing blind patriotism can be.

In Iraq we've fought, killed, and died for a handful of stupid lies eventually disavowed by those who told them. The same thing happened in Vietnam. The same thing will happen in Afghanistan.

And our soldiers' and our nation's troubles won't end when we finally leave Iraq or Afghanistan. As writer Stephen King once put it, wars don't end at treaty tables "but in cancer wards and office cafeterias and traffic jams." Wars die a piece at a time, a soldier at a time. And if our leaders make the grim decision to sacrifice our young men and women, or scramble their psyches and exhaust their humanity, all for oil and profit margins, then the sacrifice is made shabby and criminal, and our soldiers will have lived and died on distant battlefields as pawns in a villainous enterprise. The repercussions and grief will reverberate throughout our culture for generations.

Before we counsel our soldiers, then, on their resilience in the face of madness and lies, hadn't we better assess the sanity of their dispatchers?

If you tell me America has been attacked, and you send me to a country that you know had nothing to do with the attack—and have me unknowingly slaughter people who also had nothing to do with the attack—I will eventually find myself alienated from you, my community, and myself. It's one thing to be made a fool of; it's quite another to be turned into a murderer of innocents and then be discarded like shabby marionette.

As for the Army's attempts to bolster our troops' psychological resiliency in the face of such travesties, I sincerely wish them good luck. The plan obviously addresses the symptoms instead of the problem itself, but our military men and women need all the help they can get. My hope is that we don't stop there.

Our leaders need to be held accountable, and we, the public, need to be chastised for our ignorance and frightful gullibility.

In fact, as the troops receive treatment and training for their psychological maladies, we could stand to be screened for our own potential neuroses, particularly of the collective variety. Those would include the massive apathy and brainwashing through which we allowed our government to torture, kidnap, and imprison people with impunity, to feed the Bill of Rights into the shredder, and to enrich soulless, criminal corporations who trashed our reputation around the world.

Clearly, our soldiers are not the only folks whose sanity we should be concerned about.

Hmmm. I don't know. Gee. It's almost as if Saudi Arabia has something on us.

Bullies on Parade
Fort Worth Weekly February 12, 2020

A few days ago, Sam Reynolds, a 16-year-old sophomore at Arlington High School, stood up for a victim of bullying and was fatally shot by the bully, whose crime was captured on security video. Reynolds was unarmed.

Bullies don't take being challenged very well. And they usually try to make their challengers pay, so when Arlington Police Chief Will Johnson tweeted, "This senseless act of gun violence has no place in society," I almost laughed.

Excepting the friends and family who actually knew Reynolds, all the "thoughts and prayers" and the "mourning the loss of"s are arguably disingenuous. Folks who stand up to bullies are being beaten and murdered every day, but we—as a nation—really don't care, because it's usually our bullies who are doing the bullying.

One of our bullies in Saudi Arabia, for example, is the crown prince. Mohammad bin Salman recently had some of his men torture and dismember *Washington Post* journalist and American critic Jamal Khashoggi in the Saudi Consulate in Istanbul—and we turned a blind eye so we could sell the Saudis billions of dollars' worth of bombs so they can be bigger bullies. And for the last few years, we've been in bed with unabashed bully Vladimir Putin, even though it's no secret he imprisons and/or kills folks who stand up to him, in one case even poisoning expatriate detractor Alexander Litvinenko[51] with radio-nuclide polonium-210—condemning him to a horrible death by radiation poisoning that garnered worldwide headlines.

It's not always as direct as first-degree murder, of course. Sometimes it's simply state-sanctioned oppression. State governments around the nation have been overlooking the destructive tendencies of the biggest bully of all, the fossil fuel industry, for years. And this past May, Texas state senators passed legislation banning the protest of oil and gas pipelines, even if they run through your own backyard. The mere intent to protest or obstruct Big Oil's thuggish tactics could cost any concerned citizen willing to stand up to them $4,000 and a year behind bars.

Hell, unrepentant ruffian Rush Limbaugh recently received the Medal of Freedom, even though he has more blood on his hands than the last ten major American mass murderers combined, because there's little doubt that the first button on most of their car radios was tuned to whatever broadcast affiliate that aired the bully's pulpit.

No matter how well-intentioned, almost all of us screw up our kids up in one way or another. We could at least try to avoid intentionally conditioning them to be ignorant and racist.

Surviving Their Raising

Fort Worth Weekly November 12, 2008

A few weeks back, a 7th-grader who hangs around the neighborhood told my kids that Barack Obama was a stupid Muslim terrorist and that if that "nigger" got elected, he and his family were moving to Canada.

A week ago, my 10-year-old daughter related the new joke going around her elementary school: What's the difference between Obama and Simba? Simba[52] is an African lion and Obama is a lyin' African.

And the day after the election, in a high-school lunch line, a sulky-looking kid standing behind my 15-year-old son was asked by a friend what was wrong. "There's a nigger in the White House now," he said. "Yeah, I know," the friend replied. "I don't like him either."

As a parent of mixed-race children, I find the ignorance inherent in these sentiments offensive. I would find it just as revolting if my kids were white, Hispanic, or of any other ethnic background. But I'm not upset with the children who parrot such ideas. I'm unhappy with their parents.

Teenagers are not genetically predisposed to use ugly racial slurs. That kind of prejudice starts at home. Ten-year-olds don't independently question a politician's integrity or sit up thinking of ways to mock half of his ethnicity. And young middle-school students don't instinctively suspect Obama is a Muslim or equate that with being a terrorist. It's something they get from Mom or Dad—from the language routinely used at home, or the jokes repeated there, or the attitudes that, subtly or overtly, the grown-ups at home display in dealing with other people.

The "trickle-down" theory of economics may have proven to be a terrible blunder, but the moniker itself is solid. It's simply misapplied.

Wealth doesn't trickle down, but ignorance sure does.

If a child's parents are members of the Ku Klux Klan or the Aryan Nation or are simply active, vocal racists, chances are that child will absorb those repugnant ideologies and learn to discriminate against ethnic minorities. If a child's father hangs out on street corners holding up signs that say "God Hates Fags," the chances of that child becoming a homophobic bumpkin who is afraid of gay marriage increase exponentially. If Mom and Dad are shallow, xenophobic neocons who mock anyone the talk radio jocks tell them they should feel threatened by or disagree with, little Timmy is much more inclined to denigrate people who make him uncomfortable or who have different political opinions.

Hate breeds hate. So many of the evils that plague our nation— racism, sexism, homophobia, and general narrowmindedness—are passed down from grandparents to parents to kids like family pictures or precious heirlooms.

Hence, ignorance and cruelty continually dim our collective future. American poet Anne Sexton[53] put it best: "Live or die, but don't poison everything."

If you're so eaten up with hate and fear that you can't abide the skin color or free will or liberty of others, that's your prerogative. But please, do us all a favor and keep it to yourself.

No offense, but the world might be a better place if the chains of which you are a link were broken—not to mention the chains you'd like to see the rest of us wrapped in. If we could stop stuffing our children like Thanksgiving turkeys with our preconceived notions and prejudices, they might grow up to figure things out for themselves.

Trust me, as a fellow parent: For my children and yours, life is too short to make them spend years trying to transcend our follies. Let's allow them a fresh start, a clean slate. And who knows, one of our kids might grow up to be president someday.

In some states, to think is to weigh and consider and possibly understand. Or solve. To "Captain Texas" and his ilk, to think is to betray or undermine.

Ask Galileo

Unpublished April 19, 2011

Here lately, it seems like every time I pay attention to the news I'm curtly informed that kids in other countries are lapping our children in the disciplines of math and science. I hear politicians taking up rhetorical arms and pointing them at schools. I see teachers and school administrators assuming a defensive posture. Meanwhile, our children are staring out their classroom windows wondering what we'll bore them with next.

There's lots of blame to go around, but not much honesty or common sense. In fact, one of the biggest problems stifling our progeny's grasp of math and science is never even mentioned, probably because it points the finger at us instead of instructors and jeopardizes our "God-given" right to anti-intellectualism.

In August of 2006, a study published in *Science* magazine compared the beliefs and support for the Theory of Evolution in the United States, Japan, Turkey and thirty-one European countries. Of the thirty-four nations surveyed, the United States finished second to last in its acceptance of Evolution, edging out only Turkey which, truth be told, only recently achieved "First World" status.

Another study in 2006 ranked a similar list of countries in student performance in science and math and every country that acknowledged the relevance and importance of the Theory of Evolution more than the United States, scored higher in both subjects.

The implications are unavoidable. Our wishful metaphysical beliefs are stunting our intellectual development.

We once led the world in education and now we just barely edge out First World Johnny-Come-Latelies and banana republics. But it's not due to an education crisis. It's the predictable result of our culture wars.

We live in a nation where Santa Claus has more weight than Socrates and Sarah Palin trumps Stephen Hawking. We like "deciders" who walk, talk and look like us instead of articulate leaders who may be more deliberative; and we prefer personalities who "refudiate"[54] intelligent analysis and tweet their way through complex issues instead of sober, thoughtful adults who read too much and challenge our puerile sensibilities.

Our children's intellectual mediocrity is no surprise. They're as stupid, blind and ignorant as us, and we like it that way. We don't want them aspiring to serious education; it would undermine the artificial constructs that we hold so dear and expose our petty illusions. We don't send our sons and daughters to college for them to learn to think more critically or reason more carefully. We send them there to game the degree mill and land a cushy job that supports the machinery of our complacence.

We tolerate math and science until they cast doubts on our preconceived notions and challenge our conventional indoctrination. Ask Galileo.[55]

You're a genius if you cure polio or find a way to send captured images and sounds across time and space for Middle America's viewing pleasure, but if you suggest Adam wasn't shaped out of "Holy" Play-Doh or human activity may be adversely affecting the planet's ecosystems, you're an enemy of the state.

Why not just admit the truth? It's time to quit wasting everybody's time. We don't want to compete with intellectuals because we don't respect, admire or aspire to be intellectuals.

Faith is more important to us than facts and, as we have every intention of inheriting the earth, we must remain meek.

We should quit fighting ignorance and embrace it. We should build more Creation museums and convert empirical natural history displays in existing museums to illustrative Biblical interpretations. We should mandate "Flat Earth" curriculums in our schools and we should dismiss every report of climate change, global warming, animal extinctions, fresh water shortages, etc. as sheer and utter blasphemy.

It's time to bring back the ducking stool, the pillory and perhaps even the Inquisition. Smart people need to learn their place and these standardized tests that heretics harass our kids with need to be redesigned to test piety, not pensiveness.

With less intellectuals around, we would feel better about ourselves and everyone would be more agreeable. Let someone else be the brains of the planet. We just want what we want and don't want to be bothered with the consequences.

It's been a long time since we were the good guys.

Opposing Teams
Fort Worth Weekly May 30, 2018

The other day a sperm whale washed up dead on a public beach in southern Spain. When the local El Valle Wildlife Rescue Center examined the remains, they determined that the whale was killed by gastrointestinal shock after ingesting 64 pounds of plastic. The autopsy found plastic bags, nets, ropes, and sacks in the whale's stomach and intestines.

Call me crazy, but the whole story made me want to rip out my teeth and starve.

My response obviously wasn't healthy (for me, at least) or normal. But maybe it should be. Maybe the only way we're going to pull back from the brink is if our collectively destructive behavior makes us sick and suicidal. The irony, of course, is that our collective behavior is sick and suicidal.

It's true that past world leaders haven't done enough to mitigate, limit, or slow down climate change. But the United States' current White House occupant is repealing the very little that past leaders have accomplished. He's throwing out regulations on air pollutants and the disposal of toxic waste, undermining clean energy programs, doubling down on noxious energy resources, removing mentions of climate change in studies of national security threats (even though climate change-worsened natural disasters and a dwindling supply of clean natural resources are creating conflict and refugee crises), weakening threatened species guidelines (even though the alarming decrease in species diversity increasingly threatens our own species), rolling back emissions standards (even though he has no standards regarding his own emissions), and that's just the tip of the (melting) iceberg.

After 9/11, another Republican administration proffered the one percent doctrine to commence a "war" on "terror." Vice President Dick Cheney asserted, "If there's a one percent chance that Pakistani scientists are helping al-Qaeda build or develop a nuclear weapon, we have to treat it as a certainty in terms of our response. It's not about our analysis . . . It's about our response."

Later, National Security Advisor Condoleeza Rice[56] succinctly concurred, applying the paradigm to a country that had nothing to do with the 9/11 attacks: "The problem here is that there will always be some uncertainty about how quickly [Saddam Hussein] can acquire nuclear weapons. But we don't want the smoking gun to be a mushroom cloud."

So we demolished Iraq and started a war (on terror) that we will never stop paying for. Or end.

Today, however, Republicans and this Republican administration refuse—despite staggering, terrifying analysis—to even formulate a response, much less apply the one percent standard to an undeniable potential "mushroom cloud." And it's not just a political or state threat—it's a universal existential threat.

Unsurprisingly, a new one percent doctrine has emerged.

If the richest one percent—who control forty percent of the wealth in this country and fifty percent around the planet—don't want regulations that affect their profit margins or personal short-term gains, the Republicans will attack any analysis that undermines the one percent's directives and thwart efforts to ensure the safety and common good of the citizenry. It's oligarchy for all—*screw mushroom clouds!*

It's unpleasant to think on this, but it should be made plain. We can't simultaneously root for America and planet Earth right now. We're not even on the same team.

So, it's time to answer some tough questions.

Black Lives Matter, Blue Lives Matter—*does life in the oceans matter? Does the rest of life on the planet matter?* Is it too late to include Mother Earth in the #MeToo conversation?

Why does our existence make it impossible for so many other species to thrive? And, worse, why are we okay with it? Does non-human life matter? Does non-human molestation, abuse, or assault matter?

Do any lives really matter if all life doesn't matter?

Must the success of the human genome be inversely proportionate to the success of almost all other life forms on this wheezing blue orb?

Yes, I feel like ripping my teeth out.

If this is the best we can do, shouldn't you?

George Orwell is often credited with saying that "Journalism is printing what someone else does not want printed; everything else is public relations." I admire this quote, but I'm pretty sure it's a rephrasing of "If liberty means anything at all, it means the right to tell people what they do not want to hear." The latter comes from a discarded preface to Animal Farm. *I prefer writers who truly exercise liberty.*

Create Dangerously: A Call to Artistic Arms

Dissident Voice December 23, 2010

On January 19, 1919, Vaslav Nijinsky, the greatest dancer of the 20th century, performed a special wartime recital at the Suvretta House Hotel in St. Moritz, Switzerland. Leading up to the event, he refused to say what he intended to dance and wouldn't even give hints as to the accompaniment. He was, after all, a star of the highest magnitude. He influenced culture, fashion and society and his appearance would draw a crowd regardless of the presentation.

When the recital started, he performed some perfunctory turns and flashed his mastery in a few signature aerials. Then he grabbed a chair and abruptly sat down, facing his audience.

Nijinsky glared at them. Time passed but the audience was silent. More time passed and still Nijinsky stared. The audience sat motionless.

After several minutes, Nijinsky rose. He took rolls of black and white velvet and made a giant cross the length of the room. Then he stood at the head of it with open arms and said: "Now I will dance you the war, with its suffering, with its destruction, with its death. The war which you did not prevent and so you are responsible for."

And then Nijinsky erupted across the room, his monumental gestures filling the space with horror and suffering. The audience was breathless, fascinated and petrified. Nijinsky's movements and expressions suffused the room with twisted, contorted bodies and savage explosions. He took his audience to the trenches, the front and the body-strewn aftermath.

His audience was disconcerted, but undeniably moved. His recital was intense, brilliant and compelling.

If you go to the neighborhood library or check Wikipedia, you may find Nijinsky as a historical figure or a physical genius. But you will hardly find the spirit of the phenomena he represented. And it's nonexistent on the TV channels and radio stations we tune into. Taylor Swift is as challenging as a lukewarm bath. Lil Wayne is as evocative as a mustard burp. And Justin Bieber is as meaningful as bread crumbs in a jar of mayonnaise. They are devoid of urgency and sadly lack the poetic ferocity that comprised Nijinsky's St. Moritz performance.

Contemporary pop culture is virtually bereft of real relevance and depth, and the corporate architects who promote it go to extraordinary lengths to keep it that way. Sure, there's a Sinead O'Connor tearing up the Pope's picture here and there, and now and then we hear a Rage Against the Machine; but the Bob Dylans are desperately missed. There's no future in banal Beyonces, toothless Labeoufs or spineless *Twilight* and *Harry Potter* sequels.

Kurt Vonnegut used to say that artists were like canaries in a coal mine. That they were supersensitive and "keeled over" due to toxic conditions long before normal folks even sensed they were in danger. Vonnegut envisioned art as an indispensable herald, a critical means of alarm.

But despite the unparalleled toxicity of our times and our complicity in the systems that endanger us, artists aren't sounding the alarm. There are thousands of doom-impending calamities in the world, but most artists are hardly even sentient, much less supersensitive.

113

Albert Camus went further than Vonnegut. He plainly stated that "the time for irresponsible artists is over" and that in any troubled era, it was every legitimate artist's role to create dangerously.

We are involved in one war and one quasi-occupation, but no performer on any significant stage or medium is dancing the war for us, or compellingly conveying the shabbiness of the occupation. Our socio-economic system is exposing us to a catalogue of environmental perils, but our creative communities spend more time cashing in on the system than condemning it. Our technological dependence is rendering an untold number of our natural, physiological capacities obsolete, but more artists are turning to the new, dehumanizing technologies than disputing their long-term merit.

Art for art's sake was fine when there was nothing at stake, but when everything is at stake artistic expression demands courage and accountability. So, if you fancy yourself a literary or filmic or singing sort and your muse isn't telling you to dance our inhumanities or paint our self-destructiveness, maybe you should ignore it and find another pursuit among the uninitiated throngs.

We have enough artists who create safely.

She landed on her feet, parlaying her Playboy *spread into an acting career. She has appeared in* Frost/Nixon *(2008),* Alpha Males Experiment *(2009)* Dance Fu *(2011) and will apparently star in the upcoming* 3 Tickets to Paradise.

Conduct Unbecoming

Fort Worth Weekly March 7, 2007

I've been struggling with how to say this, but there's just no civil way to put it. Uncle Sam is a hypocritical, chauvinist pig.

That, I think, is the moral of Michelle Manhart's story. Last month, Manhart, a U.S. Air Force drill sergeant and 30-year-old mother of two, was demoted to senior airman and removed from active duty at Lackland Air Force Base in San Antonio. Her crime: posing in the February 2007 issue of *Playboy*.

Under the caption of "Tough Love," Manhart appeared in a six-page spread, shouting orders and holding weapons, in and out of uniform and sometimes totally nude. According to newspaper and wire service reports, Manhart believes the Air Force's decision was based on her having appeared in the magazine in military dress, not out of it—the implication perhaps being that she somehow disgraced the uniform by associating it with sexuality. "I'm disappointed with our system," she said.

Lackland Air Force Base spokesperson Oscar Balladares told reporters that Manhart's appearance in *Playboy* "does not meet the high standards we expect of our airmen, nor does it comply with the Air Force's core values of integrity, service before self, and excellence in all we do."

I just have two questions. How many copies of the February 2007 issue of *Playboy* were delivered to military personnel at Lackland Air Force Base and to American military bases around the world? And, speaking of "service before self," how many military personnel have serviced themselves utilizing *Playboy* photos of Manhart?

Oh, my mistake. All those soldiers just subscribe to *Playboy* and *Hustler* and *Penthouse* for the excellent editorial coverage, right?

Before the Air Force higher-ups put on white gloves, shouldn't they come clean? If posing for *Playboy* is behavior unbecoming to military personnel, then shouldn't lasciviously ogling nude women in *Playboy* constitute behavior unbecoming to military personnel as well?

And this raises other issues. Don't most overseas American military bases lie in conspicuous proximity to popular prostitution industries? Isn't it common knowledge that male military personnel often while away significant stretches of R & R in strip joints, exotic dance clubs, and brothels? Is the integrity of these men questioned? Are they demoted for their lechery—or are servicemen who frequent foreign whorehouses upholding the military's "core values of integrity?"

Indulging in the skin trade has long been a traditional military rite of passage—so much so that the prostitution trade surrounding American air bases in Thailand during the Vietnam war helped create the prostitution industry so rampant in that country today. Are male soldiers, sailors, and airmen even discouraged by their superiors from sampling local brothels?

I'm not a fan of *Playboy*. I think it's lame and silly, and I wouldn't want my wife or daughter posing for the masculine legions (military or civilian) that gape through it every month. But Manhart is a responsible adult. And nothing she could do in *Playboy* could make the morale of our military forces any worse than it already is. Truth be told, couldn't Manhart's appearance in a nudie mag actually, well, *stiffen* their resolve?

During the 1991 invasion of Iraq, top U.S. General Stormin' Norman Schwarzkopf[57] called *Playboy*'s "Operation Playmate" a "major morale boost" for the troops, lauding the publication for its war efforts. "Operation Playmate" encouraged male GI's to write to their favorite centerfolds who in turn sent admiring troops autographed photos of themselves in bathing suits or halter tops.

Does the Air Force realize that *Playboy* re-launched "Operation Playmate" in 2003? Does the Air Force condone the fact that GIs are soliciting the attention of *Playboy* playmates as we speak?

Not that posing in or perusing the pages of skin mags is the military's worst personnel problem—not even close.

Uncle Sam recently relaxed the high standards he for years demanded in terms of military recruitment. According to news reports, the Army is now accepting twice as many recruits with felonies and serious misdemeanors on their records as it did in 2003. And American armed forces in general are now increasingly faced with the necessity of accepting less than desirable recruits to maintain the human element of this nation's military industrial complex and keep it chugging right along.

Moreover, the *Hartford Courant* recently won a major award for an investigative report revealing that mentally unfit troops are more and more often being kept in or re-deployed to war zones and offered powerful drugs to keep their instability under control—while receiving little or no counseling.

Clearly, Uncle Sam has bigger problems than Michelle Manhart taking her camos off in *Playboy*. But I guess when he says "I Want You," he's more often referring to horny male felons and the mentally unstable, not to bold, exhibitionist women.

As our most recent, billionaire dick wag demonstrates, American politicians are more committed to allowing the obscenely wealthy to dip their manicured toes into the space than seeing the typical citizen earn a living wage.

Taxing Nonsense

Unpublished November 18, 2011

It's hard not to cringe when people talk about the ninety percent income tax rate on wealthy folks under President Eisenhower. Or the seventy percent income tax rate on the well-off under presidents Nixon through Carter. They seem outrageous and unfair, almost un-American. But the economies under those leaders were good. And under Ike the economy was vibrant and prosperous. The United States was winning, and higher taxes on the wealthy played a big part.

I know the very mention of taxing "job creators" cuts conservative flesh to the bone and sends victims scurrying to their flat-screens for the salve of countermanding *Fox News* talking points—but hear me out. We're being had and this is no time to gather up our toyed-with outlooks on this issue and run home.

President Eisenhower and presidents Nixon through Carter weren't taxing the rich to punish them; they were taxing them to build the economy. And wealthy folks who were highly taxed still got handsomely rewarded.

"You lie" is a popular conservative response—but I don't lie.

"How?" you ask (hardly masking your incredulity, if not outright contempt) could the aforementioned economies have prospered under such oppressive tax rates?

That should be obvious. Especially to businesspeople.

Deductions.

When the wealthy and well-off in this country were taxed at such exorbitant rates under Eisenhower and Nixon, they didn't pay exorbitant taxes. They utilized every deduction and write-off in the book. Like any other red-blooded American entrepreneur, they wrote off everything possible and rewarded themselves and their companies every way they could. They bought new equipment and increased their business's assets. They paid for company vacations, yachts, vehicles, etc. They gave out extra employee bonuses. These expenditures were all tax-deductible investments that essentially constituted back-door rewards. Higher taxes didn't punish the wealthy because they didn't pay them.

Higher taxes led to greater deductions. Greater deductions led to increased investment and commercial expansion. Increased investment and expansion created higher GDP.

This is not rocket science. Where our overall economy is concerned, higher taxes create greater investment and lower taxes achieve exactly the opposite.

Lower taxes reduce deductions. Decreased deductions stifle spending and subdue investment. Lower taxes enable wealthy folks to sock away their profits instead of investing them in the economy. Put simply, the most effective way to shrink the middle class is to allow the wealthy to hoard the profits they've garnered largely from the backs of the middle class.

Higher taxes will never force the Tea Party's capitalist "Atlases" to shrug—they're already being allowed to shrug by lower taxes. And the ridiculous Grover Norquist[58] anti-tax chastity pledge is simply an iatrogenic measure that further endangers an already reeling patient. It keeps investment and spending low and misery high.

I am not wealthy, so this isn't going to be a Joe the Plumber[59] mischaracterization. I am involved in a small business. If we have a good year and it looks like we'll have to pay more taxes, we simply buy a new company truck or computer or some other useful piece of equipment or inventory. The company I work for still pays taxes, but also pays itself. The write-off is good, and it puts money back into the economy. The better investments we make, the better the economy does. Every good businessman (or woman) should know this.

If we're truly in this together, trying to get this country back on its feet and move it forward, aren't higher tax-spurred deductions a good thing?

They worked for Ike, and he had WWII to pay for.

The anti-tax mantra is anti-progress in terms of the problems we face. The burgeoning deficit will not be reduced by lower taxes. The middle class will not be restored by lower taxes.

It's time to look to the Greatest Generation for solutions. President Eisenhower's higher taxes forced the wealthy to spend instead of hoard. Higher taxes today would do the same, and the wealthy would still be wealthy.

I'm not ashamed of my whiteness . . . but I am disgusted and ashamed of a lot of white folks.

Breaking Adolph Hitler's Wet Dream
Fort Worth Weekly July 16, 2021

As a normal white guy who grew up with the normal white bread breaks, I have to say I'm pretty fed up with listening to other white guys complain about how put-upon they are.

By normal breaks, I mean I wasn't born with a silver spoon up my arse like George W. Bush or Donald J. Trump. Oh, and my parents weren't politicians or multi-millionaires, so I wouldn't have been able join the Texas National Guard or get a medical deferment from a friendly doctor to avoid serving in Vietnam. I enjoyed the normal breaks. You know, the ones that almost anybody who didn't look like me rarely got.

For all practical purposes, I was Adolph Hitler's wet dream. I was blonde-haired, blue-eyed (well, actually hazel, but close enough for government work), athletic and, oh yeah, white. One Saturday, as a preteen—while visiting my uncle in Fort Worth—I threw rocks through several school windows adjacent to a playground I was playing at. In broad daylight. One of the school maintenance men, who lived next door to the school, heard the breaking glass and accosted me with a shotgun. I told him I thought I'd seen a ghost. He kept the shotgun trained on me till the police arrived. They brought a paddy wagon out just to scare me, I think, but my uncle paid for the damage and there were never any charges filed.

As a teenager, some friends and I borrowed the fire extinguishers off every school bus in our town one Halloween, and drove around spraying people with them. The high school principal and a county sheriff's deputy confronted us the next school day and, after unsuccessfully bracing us regarding the missing fire safety equipment, agreed to not press charges or inform our parents if I led them to the empty spray cannisters, which I promptly did.

I suspect our principal may have been concerned about the buses being operated without extinguishers, so we probably got lucky. And that didn't slow us down. We also absconded with our school statue, "streaked" in front the local Holy Rollers, played several innings of mailbox baseball, were serial ding-dong ditchers, etc., etc., etc.

As a grown man—the same day my father died in a Fort Worth hospital—I followed my mother home in my truck. She entered the house first through the garage and I came in through the front door. Understandably shaken, she forgot to disable her alarm system. When the alarm sounded, she promptly disabled it, but the local police didn't get the message. I was sitting on her couch, changing the channels of her TV with a black remote control. We heard a car pull up outside, and my mother said it might be the police, but I was already at the front door. I stepped out with the black remote control in hand.

"FREEZE!" a panicked voice screamed, before I even looked up.

It was a local cop, firearm drawn and gun barrel trained on me. He was fifty feet away at least, and there I was, holding a dark object in my right hand. It happened so fast I hadn't had time to think. And I didn't consider that if it was actually the police, my unhailed exit with an identifiable dark object in my right hand—and probably a scowl on my face, because my father had just died—was probably a terrible idea.

But it was okay.

I was Adolph Hitler's wet dream, a blonde-haired member of the Master Race. A white man with all the normal breaks.

Now, I know what all you self-identified, put-upon white men are thinking. All this stuff is anecdotal, it doesn't prove anything.

But you're mistaken.

For starters, for most of this country's existence, black children and black teenagers weren't permitted to be juvenile in public, much less juvenile delinquents. It was beat out of them with a whip or corrected at the end of a rope. And a grown, black man barging out of a house in the suburbs with police officers out front, holding an unidentified black object in his hands and wearing a scowl on his face? Well, I'm sure you don't need to see the statistics on what often comes next.

But it's not just about race—even though every disgruntled Hitler's wet dream I know tries to make it so.

Women—like my own mother—weren't: (1) allowed to serve on juries in all fifty states until 1973; (2) weren't permitted to have their own credit cards until 1974 (Thanks, Ruth Bader Ginsburg!); (3) weren't able to get pregnant without fear of getting fired for it until 1978; (4) weren't eligible to pursue a college education at all eight Ivy League schools until 1981; and (5) weren't allowed to safely say, "Not tonight, dear, I have a headache," until 1993. And twenty-eight years later we're still trying to make their birth control decisions for them.

The original Hitler at least had the good sense to blow his brains out.

White men in America don't even have brains enough to stay out of everybody's way.

Isolating a deadly contagion is always best.

We Don't Deserve Another Planet

Dissident Voice February 20th, 2012

I'm scared. I worry a lot.

I'm afraid for our future. I'm afraid for our species.

I'm afraid *of* our species.

Homo Sapiens corrupt or foul any ecosystem that lies in the path of their economic interests. *Homo Sapiens* marginalize and/or exterminate almost every species of fellow inhabitant that it comes into contact with. Homo Sapiens are defiling the gasping blue orb they call home, but they press on almost entirely heedless of their loathsome wrongheadedness.

You, me and every human being up and down our street, across the nation and throughout the world, en masse, comprise a sinister planetary menace. It is not our intent; we just can't or won't control ourselves.

Fort Worth writer and former resident John Graves[60] once said that human beings would be finished when they stopped "understanding the old pull toward green things and living things." But we're already there. We are monstrously out of sync with the natural world. We no longer even take part in the most basic facets of our own sustenance.

Technology has replaced survival processes with leisure. Our livelihoods are based on ancillary subsistence modes which translate into petty barter for factory farming and mechanized industrial slaughter. We live on pre-processed pseudo-nourishment. We reside in prefabricated shelters bathed in artificial light, and filled with conditioned air. We don't thrive as vital, fully-functional creatures; we merely exist as detached bystanders.

In our natural state we were never idle or bored or prone to weight gains due to a sedentary lifestyle. We were constantly involved in the means of survival, hands-on, acute and in-tune. We didn't need Vegas or roller coasters or Viagra. Every day was a gamble and every food-source capture or kill was a victory if not an outright adrenaline rush. In our present state we struggle to survive business as usual with any useful, natural instincts intact.

Several seconds before the late August 2011 earthquake near the National Zoo in DC, flamingos grouped together, upper mammals climbed trees and lemurs sounded alarm calls. In our early existence, we probably weren't much different than the spooked animals at the National Zoo. We probably sensed phenomena like earthquakes at an elemental level, before they happened, because we were more in touch with our habitat. Truth be told, we arguably knew more then as preyed-upon primitives than we know now as reckless louts at the top of the food chain.

We are a species run amok, obtuse and self-destructive. It's time to debate Capitalism in a world of limited resources; it's time to have a referendum on unaccountable Technology. If the swift-shod proliferation of excessive consumption in the name of ever-increasing profit margins reduces humanity to a lethal scourge, Capitalism is an evil that can no longer be tolerated. If the unavoidable byproducts of technology are human overpopulation, the pollution or contamination of our air, water and food supplies, biological exploitation and artificial preservation—all created at the expense of the planet and our fellow species—Technology is an evil that can no longer be promoted. If Capitalism and Technology cannot be practiced with conscience, then we cannot conscientiously engage in them.

These issues warrant debate in the fore of this historical moment because humankind is toying with the notion of exploring and/or colonizing other earth-like planets in their galactic vicinity. It's one thing for us to plunder and savage our own home. It's quite another to destroy someone else's home.

We must stop averting our eyes. We need to quit ignoring our crimes. In the grand scheme of things, we've become a vicious virus that should be isolated and confined, allowing our madness to run its course, come what may.

As bad as things stand on Earth for inhabitants other than *Homo Sapiens*, at least *Homo Sapiens* are contained here. And the fledgling life-support and propulsion technologies that keep us from exploring deep-space ensure our quarantine.

If we perish, our perilous, suicidal propensities should die with us and not be flung amongst the stars to infect or endanger other living systems. The species *Homo Sapiens* had its chance.

Tragically, we're wasting it.

Sorry folks, I call 'em like I see 'em.

God Works in Mistaken Ways
Dissident Voice November 25th, 2008

Much has been made of late regarding the theory of evolution and how it's taught in Texas public schools. For the next few months, the Texas State Board of Education will be considering changes to our children's science curricula. The chairman of this board, a dentist named Don McLeroy, calls himself a Creationist and believes in a literal reading of the Bible. Cynthia Dunbar, a vocal board member, recently made news when she suggested that in the first six months of Barrack Obama's presidential administration, he would collude with terrorists to bring down our nation.

I don't know about you, but I wouldn't trust a biblical literalist, much less an admitted Creationist to arrange my children's sock drawer, much less instruct, presume to choose who instructs or definitively decide what gets instructed to my children in a public school setting, much less a science classroom. And Mrs. Dunbar—a conservative zealot who is so thoroughly brainwashed that she (according to her own website) believes that her role on the Board of Education includes ferreting out nefarious "socialist" and "humanist" agendas—has absolutely no business proposing or voting on anyone's intellectual future, let alone our children's.

To date, a State Board of Education committee recommended a "change" in our public school curriculum that allows for an examination of the "strengths and limitations" of the theory of evolution in regards to the instruction of biology and science. This is simply the first step toward allowing Christian Creationist operatives to insert their mythology into public school curricula—it has nothing to do with real science or the instruction thereof. But for the sake of argument, let's settle this once and for all.

It's really simple. Like most scientific theories, evolution is based on and bolstered by the scientific method.

Formulate a question. Research and observe. Form a hypothesis. Perform an experiment. Collect and analyze data. Interpret data and draw conclusions. Reproduce and verify data. Publish your findings. The scientific method is universal and inviolate. Every serious branch of science has roots in it. Any conclusions arrived at by the scientific method are open to all takers. They can be tested, disputed, challenged and/or refuted if demonstrable, empirical evidence suggests a claim or theory is flawed or unsound.

The theory of evolution is the scientific heavyweight of explanations for humanity's origins because it's the most challenged, tested, supported and applied theory that anyone anywhere has ever come up with on the subject. Evolutionary principles are the foundation on which the studies of biology, botany, zoology, pathology, medicine, etc. are established. Without them, you, me and the esteemed members of our State Board of Education would still be having our blood drawn by leeches when we paid a visit to our local physician.

Creationist narratives for human evolution are based on faith instead of science, and hold up only to adherents of said faith whom invariably claim their beliefs require no scientific evidence or demonstrable proofs. And there's just one enormous, unavoidable problem with that: in any legitimate forum devoted to the origin of our species, the line for proponents of Creationist narratives starts at the back door and winds around the planet. Who decides who's right?

The Bantu tribes of central Africa believe a god named Bumba regurgitated the sun, moon, stars, and human beings after a bad tummy-ache. The Scandinavian creation narrative maintains that humans descended from frost giants which emerged from the dripping underarm sweat of an evil ogre named Ymir. Persian Zoroastrians held that the first humans grew out of a rhubarb plant. The ancient Chinese believed that the goddess Numa shaped humans out of mud from the Yellow River because she was lonely. The Japanese creation narrative suggests that a goddess named Izanami and a god named Izanagi created the first Earthen land mass by stirring the ocean with a bejeweled spear until it curdled. Inuit Eskimos believe the world was formed by a raven.

It doesn't matter to me if you and I are actually descended from vomit, sweaty armpits, rhubarbs, curdled ocean, mud or dust; until such claims can be reasonably traced, observed, tested and verified they do not constitute "science" and therefore do not belong in a "science" curriculum.

I have no problem with my kids being taught Creationist narratives because each one has its own cultural richness and contains clues to each people's prehistoric, oral traditions. It's fascinating, profound stuff, but the tales themselves fall under the heading of anthropology, not science (or biology). And until these narratives can be scientifically validated, it should never be otherwise.

In the Christian creation narrative, after God reportedly created Adam, he is said to have explicitly instructed, "Of every tree of the garden thou mayest freely eat: But of the tree of Knowledge of good and evil, thou shall not eat of it: for in the day thou eatest thereof *thou shalt surely die*" (italics mine).

Adam ate of this tree and did not die.

God was wrong.

Regarding the eminence of evolution in our public schools, so are many of his current followers.

I'm not sure that this isn't anything we don't already know, deep down, but we refuse to admit it. We seem incapable of facing it and, worse, acting accordingly.

Sit Down

Fort Worth Weekly January 29, 2020

We need to have a talk.

A real, down-to-earth, grown-up talk.

But not with the kids.

We need to have a grown-up talk with the grown-ups.

People like us—adults, parents, grandparents, even great-grandparents—we've lived our lives mostly optimistically and, regardless of religion (or irreligion), with one shared article of faith: that we were working toward progress and, specifically, that each new generation would have things better than the last. Better lives. Better opportunities. Better tools. Better rules. And a brighter future. It's been a staple of most of our existences. It's been a goal and an ongoing process, and—regardless of our politics or worldview—we've all coalesced around our simple faith in it. We have been united by this dream and committed to this wonderful aspiration.

Unfortunately, however, we have also been blinded by it. We believe it is simply part of our DNA. We seem unable to acknowledge that it is no longer possible.

By the time the Baby Boomers[61] were in their 30s, well into careers, raising kids, and settling into adulthood, blue-collar wages were great. The average journeyman electrician, for example, made just over $20 an hour. It was a comfortable, living wage for important work. The typical automobile at that time cost $3,000, and the average home ran around $15,000. Today, the hourly wage for the average journeyman electrician is still just over $20—but the typical automobile costs $36,000 and the standard home $200,000.

This is the state of the American dream. Most American citizens are upside down in terms of their finances and basically live check to check.

The next generation isn't going to have or enjoy or afford nearly as much as the Baby Boomers did. The next generation isn't going to be able to have or enjoy or afford as much as Generation X did. Put it out of your mind. We all had more, and they're going to have less. And their lesser spoils aren't even going to be real, satisfying, or healthy.

While we were growing up, starting lives, having kids, and engaged in careers, we could, for the most part, at least count on a significant portion of the food on our tables being real, naturally occurring, produced without gobs of preservative byproducts, created without genetic modification, pumped full of growth hormones or antibiotics, or sprayed with poisons. Today, current and future food stores are shot, and our children, grandchildren, and great-grandchildren will consume foodstuff that contains known carcinogens as a matter of course—and be happy to do so. Because there isn't enough left to go around, and things will get worse.

The generations to come will not enjoy breathing clean air.

The generations to come will not drink clean water.

And, unlike so many of us, who, after lives of safe, unremarkable sedimentary posts in the employ of corporate conglomerates who promised pension plans and retirement savings (and partially delivered), the generations to come will not even be able to retire, much less fund retirement.

We tell our children and grandchildren to pursue the same surrenders we did, spend the bulk of their adult lives in various endeavors of corporate inertia, but their payoff will not come. We're well aware of the chipping away of pensions and retirement plans today—we know that they won't be around in the near future. But we don't have time to worry about that and can't afford to tell the truth about it to our children. If they stopped buying into the lie and refused to reduce themselves to the fleecing we took, our retirement plans would be disrupted.

This dream is dead. This goal is no longer achievable. Our descendants will inherit our folly.

But we still deserve ours, right?

We smile and say everything is going to be OK, but it will not.

It's almost funny. No, it's actually intensely sad.

In 2003, we were led to war en masse over a fractional potentiality. Our leaders told us if there was a one-percent chance that another leader had nuclear weapons, we must act, we must take up arms. Because the smoking gun could be a mushroom cloud. Because we couldn't afford to take that chance. Because we couldn't ignore that infinitesimally small possibility.

Today—quite conveniently—we see things differently. Today, there's only a one-percent chance we'll survive climate change unscathed, whole cities sunk, massive swaths of entire continents reduced to desert, whole natural food sources vanished, and catalogs of entire species disappearing before our eyes.

And yet we—and especially the grown-ups—refuse to act at all.

The smoking gun is a smoking blue orb, and the second-hand "smoke" from fossil fuels is choking us all. The smoking gun is the dead zones appearing where our poisoned rivers meet the rising seas. The smoking gun is the continent-sized garbage patches in our oceans, the dying coral reefs, the reliance on genetically modified food sources, food source cloning, rising sea temperatures, longer drought seasons, killer heat waves, the increasing severity of natural disaster damage, and so much more. A hellscape for the generations to follow. A better life for no one except grown-ups today, right now, until the consequences of our ignorance and wishful thinking are writ cataclysmically large.

And yet you and I still manage to sleep at night.

And yet you and I still manage to look at ourselves in the mirror without contempt.

And you and I go back to the football games on TV or the latest binge-watch on cable.

Grown-ups.

The most shameless fools in human history. And the last comfortable adults in our bloodlines.

On January 13, 2002, President George W. Bush passed out in the White House after getting a pretzel lodged in his throat while watching a football game. Besides a scrape and a bruise on his face (from falling off a couch), he was none the worse for wear, so I promptly considered organizing a pretzel drive that would send hundreds if not thousands of bags of pretzels to 1600 Pennsylvania Avenue—to demonstrate my "support," of course.

Uncle Ahab's Blood Money

Dissident Voice December 17, 2005

I was thirty when I got married. After college, I enjoyed single life for several years. Most of my married friends were always quizzing me about who I was dating, trying to set me up with one of their friends or asking me when I might settle down. I look back now and realize the old "misery loves company" cliché perfectly described their concern. It's like they were recruiters for a weighty, tedious and sometimes perilous commitment. I'm glad it took me so long to listen.

I bring this anecdote up because the United States National Guard has adopted my old married friends' earnest, but misguided strategy. They recently initiated a test run (in Kentucky, Iowa, Missouri, North Dakota and West Virginia) of the Guard Recruiter Assistance Program, which encourages current Guard members to recruit friends, family, co-workers, fellow church members, etc. to sign up for the National Guard. If the test run is successful, the Guard Recruiter Assistance Program will expand nationwide by September 2006. This means the shrinking, shallow pools that our current National Guard taps to fight our fossil fuel crusades and lofty Operation Blah-Blah-Blahs will be re-tapped for future incursions.

I guess that makes most of us lucky. The same poor families and communities that stomached the brunt of the casualties and hardships during the War in Iraq will bear the largest measure of future misdirected hostilities and keep the United States military-industrial complex chugging right along. It's standard fare under the Bush White House; the privileged get richer and the downtrodden get poorer. Or dead. They do the bulk of the fighting and dying while we program I-pods and vegetate in front of the latest "reality" TV show.

To sweeten this dour recruiting campaign the National Guard is dangling some gainful incentives. They'll be paying National Guard members $1,000 for each new enlisted recruit and an additional $1,000 when that potential recruit reports for basic training. If a National Guardsmen enlists and lands five new recruits, he or she earns $10,000!

It obviously smacks of blood money and bad taste, but it's a nifty two-tier pyramid scheme that could bring the folks and families who are fighting our battles some financial relief, and that's good. But what does it say about the rest of us and our support for this war?

Is recruiting so bad that we have to grease our soldiers' hands to sell it? What happened to all those patriotic cars and trucks cruising around with a "W" on their back windshield? Don't they know anybody who wants to fight this war? They were damn proud to support and pay tribute to the guy who got us into this mess. Don't they want to help him clean it up?

Obviously, Uncle Sam is a scary guy these days. His red, white and blue stovetop hat is crumpled and dingy. His coat is faded and threadbare. His beard is patchy and his teeth are yellow. His skin is gaunt and his eyes are dark and sunken. When he points and says, "I want you," it's no wonder young people turn and run. He no longer inspires confidence. He looks like a ridiculous, crude incarnation of the Fourth of July. He looks like a decrepit old Captain Ahab, haunted and insanely obsessed by this great white whale of a war.

One step forward, three steps back.

Whistling Dixie

Fort Worth Weekly August 20, 2014

This is a strange time in American history. I don't recognize us.

And by us, I mean white people.

We seethe with hatred. We're fed up and embittered. Things aren't going our way, and somebody needs to pay. Someone deserves blame.

Our better angels have flown the coop, and our inner demons are at the wheel. On a daily basis, whole legions of us prostrate ourselves before hateful messiahs who spray inane vitriol, and we clamor for more.

I'm not convinced that it's even happening on a conscious level. For millions of Americans, I fear, this has become a reflex, conditioned by incessant guilt and self-loathing.

The history of slavery in this country is reprehensible. It was an unconscionable monstrosity. We don't like to think about the reality of it, the depravity that allowed it to flourish, or the fact that half the country was willing to die to defend it. Here in Texas we even threw over our own George Washington—Sam Houston himself—after he refused to lead us gently into that "good" Confederacy, which he saw as a horrific mistake. Two dozen Texas counties and thousands of sober folks sided with Houston, but he lost. Houston's woeful banishment and Texas' subsequent descent into the Civil War are hardly taught in our history books, much less touched on in serious conversation.

A century and a half has gone by, and we like to think (rather wishfully) that all is forgotten or can be forgotten. We insist it's time to move on, but we want to do so without ever having truly examined our slave-owning past.

Electing a black president made us feel a little better until we realized we had actually elected a black president. A representative of the victims of our vilest monstrosity had risen to the highest office in the land, the most powerful job in the world. While we were busy proclaiming racism dead, this young, black Gen-X president was a constant reminder of what we had labored tirelessly to forget. And he was tasked with attempting to lead us through a perilous patch, fraught with dangers domestic, foreign and economic.

When the opposition party decided to make the race card part of its political platform, it quickly legitimized our conscious and unconscious unease with the memories that Barack Obama nudged us to confront. This unease helped promote Obama's vilification and encouraged us to feel nostalgic for (or at least more comfortable with) the good ol' days when our past wasn't considered a monstrosity and racial prejudice was a point of pride.

History will judge our current lapse unmercifully.

Our internal and often external backlash to Barrack Obama's presidency is beginning to manifest itself in shocking ways. If we didn't have a black president, we wouldn't be vowing to "take our country back." If we didn't have a black president, we wouldn't be showing up at town halls and Home Depots with guns (as if we were about to try and take our country back). If our president wasn't black, George Zimmerman would have been held accountable for the murder of Trayvon Martin.

And, I fear, if the leader of the "free" world wasn't a black man, unarmed black folks wouldn't be getting shot down in cold blood by militarized law enforcement officers.

White can't be right if a black president is okay, right? And if we can't take our conscious or unconscious frustrations out on him, we can take them out on folks who look like him.

For centuries, killing black folks in this country was hardly even illegal. Now that a black man is president, our primary preoccupation is condemning everything he does and buying more guns.

Sounds like we're whistling Dixie again.

This aggression will not stand, man. —Jeff Lebowski, *The Big Lebowski*

The Scruffy American

Fort Worth Weekly May 15, 2013

Sometimes I lie awake at night and ponder odd things. Usually it happens when my slumber has been interrupted in the small hours by a stray noise, a passing train, or a disagreement with something I ate. Then there's a thought in my head, and I wonder if it's the thought itself that woke me. Usually the musings are utter nonsense; but occasionally they're genius—as much as anything one thinks about at three or four in the morning can be genius.

The other night it was a Jeff Bridges meditation lying in wait for me. I've always liked Jeff Bridges. I liked him in *The Last Picture Show*, *Thunderbolt and Lightfoot*, *Starman* and *True Grit*, and even in that corny, '80s flick *Against All Odds*. But what I probably liked the most was his '90s portrayal of Jeff Lebowski in the classic *The Big Lebowski*. In fact, when I struggled awake thinking about America and Jeff Bridges, "Lebowski" was the only name I could put to him.

Eventually, as my mind cleared, I could see Bridges' face and his characters, but I still couldn't conjure his last name: The two Jeffs had melded for a brilliant stretch of celluloid magic. The image transcended their separate realities.

The whole lapse was reminiscent of what folks used to call typecasting. Many classic cases involve actors being pigeonholed in one role and no longer being offered other kinds of parts. Think (if you're as old as me) of Bob Denver as Gilligan, Leonard Nimoy as Spock, or Adam West as Batman.

By this time, it felt like I might be on to something. I turned on the bedside lamp and tried to trap the thought on a notepad. Here it is: America has the same problem in the international consciousness that Lebowski—I mean Bridges—had for me in those garbled moments of semi-consciousness.

The new millennium has not been kind to America. Perhaps better said, America has not been kind in the new millennium.

The images of America that play across the big screen of international perception these days are mostly negative, no matter what script we're censoring or spinning to boost our national self-esteem. Even with more progressive White House leadership, we look like a sad, predictable, failing empire, cranking up the old military-industrial complex for one last push, one so prolonged that it will keep us in charge even as our most admirable qualities fade and we devolve into a scruffy, debauched has-been.

In the opening scenes of this new millennium we've played wrong-headed warmonger, ruthless torturer, greedy banker, xenophobic bigot, anti-intellectual lout, easy assassin and pathetic gun-nut. And woven through them all: sedentary, flaccid climate-change denier.

We play detestable villains so convincingly that it seems as if this might not be an act. Though we may have taken these parts because we were afraid or desperate, the rest of the planet now associates us with those images, and they may haunt us for years to come, typecasting us as a bunch of bumpkins who aren't ready for prime time, much less modern times.

This is a turn that Americans should not abide. We have more range than we've heretofore displayed. We're not just Democrats and Republicans or conservatives and liberals. We're no more Rush Limbaugh than we are Michael Moore[62] or Keith Olbermann.[63] We can do "smart and responsible." We're capable of "compassionate and reasonable." Heck, we even have "compromise" in our repertoire.

Can't we start acting like it?

OK, back to sleep. See you in the morning . . .

Hard to argue with Randolph Bourne.[64]

The S(pl)urge: Of Course It's Working
Dissident Voice July 26th, 2008

Every day John McCain[65] chastises Barrack Obama for his original stance on "The Surge."[66] McCain says Obama said the surge wouldn't work and was bald-faced wrong. Obama says the surge has been effective, but there were other factors involved.

What's suspicious about Obama's response is that it trusts the American people to ponder those other factors. Obama could come right out and enumerate them, and John McCain and even General David Petraeus would have egg on their faces. The other factors are not a secret; they're simply embarrassing because they expose the success of the surge to ridicule and pessimism.

I commend Obama for taking the high ground, but there's not enough room for all of us in the thin air, and I think it's time we spoke frankly about the Bush Administration's most effective secret weapon.

All you need to know about the "surge" is that it should have been called the "splurge." Sure, we sent 30,000 extra troops to Iraq, but during the first six months of the operation, violence went up, not down. As Retired Army Colonel Douglas McGregor put it, "Up until that point, the surge was simply providing more targets for the insurgents to shoot at."

Under extreme pressure to produce results and fill less body bags, General Petraeus cut deals with armies of enemy combatants. These deals, now part of what is referred to as the Concerned Local Citizens program, simply pay insurgents to become temporary allies of the U. S. military. Approximately 70,000 former enemy combatants are now paid to play nice and all it costs us is $700,000 a day.

That's right. For $255 million a year, 70,000 IED-planting, sniper-firing, roadside-booby-trapping insurgents will be our friends and the death toll will drop and we can pat ourselves on the back because the "surge" is working, or at least paying off in better press.

Curiously, conservatives, Republicans and Neocons are notorious for their contempt and opposition toward hand-outs. As they strut around golf courses and hunting lodges, martinis in hand, they grandly extol the merits of pulling one's self up by his or her own bootstraps. These days, however, they're polishing the boots of our heretofore enemies in Iraq and giving them per diem hand-outs so we can look like we're no longer fumbling over our own bootstraps.

Now I'm usually loath to get behind any conservative, Republican or Neocon ideas, but I like this one. It's an excellent flip-flop. In fact, I recommend we apply it to more of our problems.

So far this year, our federal, state and local governments have spent $56 billion on the War on Drugs and arrested just over one million drug law offenders. That amounts to $56,000 per offender, not including long-term incarceration costs. Why not pay offenders to clean up and stand on the sidelines? A few years of college and a pimpin' ride with 20' titanium rims would cost less than fifty-six large. And our courtrooms would be less log-jammed and our prisons would be less overcrowded.

Instead of vilifying, chasing down and prosecuting illegal aliens, why not just pay them to stay home? Mexicans abroad sent $23 billion home in 2006 and even with the housing market slump and the American economy flailing, they'll probably send at least $15 billion home this year. I say double their 2006 homeward remittances and start mailing checks to their residences in Mexico. It would be cheaper than trying to catch and prosecute them, or station troops on our border or build border walls, right?

Each Iraqi insurgent we're paying off will receive $3,640 this year (plus bragging and thumbing-his-nose-at-the-U.S. rights). That's six times more than each of us received in George W. Bush's measly economic stimulus package. And it doesn't even account for our higher cost of living expenses or inflation. I think we're being ripped off.

We're stateside "Concerned Local Citizens" and if President Bush and John McCain want us to keep voting Republican, pledging allegiance to Exxon Mobile and Fannie Mae and Freddie Mac and condemning homosexuality and comparing Obama with Nazis, they better ante up.

Lots of folks in this country say that money is what makes the world go round. The Bush Administration is clearly proof of that, but they're thinking too small. It's time to spread the wealth. If we're gonna pretend to be happy and sit idly by while they continue to screw everything up, the least they could do is compensate us accordingly.

It's the smart play. And it'll make their war against us go much more smoothly.

Don't mess with Texas—*unless it pays well.*

What Will the Kids Get?

Fort Worth Weekly October 26, 2011

About 470 years ago, famed Spanish explorer Francisco Vazquez de Coronado and his men got lost in the Texas panhandle and floundered there for three weeks. They were confounded by the endless plains. They were disoriented by a landmark-less sea of grass.

Recently, I ventured west on a Texas county road toward Palo Duro Canyon, crossing what used to be part of those amazing plains. The endless, indigenous grasslands are mostly gone. The area is now farmland.

The beginning and end of the stretch I drove was dotted with houses, metal churches, and closed-down firework stands. The middle featured wide expanses of shorn cotton fields and ember-like splashes of maize crops, some fenced, some not. There were at least two ancient buffalo wallows along the way, if you knew what you were looking for, and now and again I saw a disenfranchised coyote sneak across the road in broad daylight, with more of his brethren dead on the side of the road.

On the rare occasion that I saw a break in the crops and fences, I found myself gazing quizzically out across a patch of grassland, just like Coronado did. But it never lasted.

It's frightening to consider how quickly and utterly we've filled these wild expanses. Not quite five centuries ago, no one would have imagined it possible. But in the blink of an eye, really, we've done it. And sometimes we have the nerve to call it progress.

Out at Palo Duro, folks are building subdivisions practically right up to the canyon edges. Wild, untamable places are turning out to be docile and wobbly in the path of human "civilization" and technology. And the frontier that was first sliced up by fences is now scarred by highway asphalt, so we can reach those less-and-less-wild places faster. We can now visit most of Texas from the comfort of fully enclosed, air-conditioned, rolling bio-systems, with power windows and GPS on board. We can even cross these once mythical expanses without even noticing them, which was maybe the goal all along.

There are still a few spots where we can get lost, but they're shrinking as fast as our water supply. The wild stretches in the Big Bend region come to mind and the forests and thickets of the Piney Woods area. But I fear for them too.

We like to talk about pride here in Texas, but some of the ways we've exploited our lands are nothing to be proud of. Andrews County out west of Big Spring now hosts a 1,338-acre dump for low-grade nuclear waste. The Great State of Texas now allows thirty-six other (once considered lesser) states to dump their nuclear waste here, and the dump sits in the precarious vicinity of our massive, precious Ogallala Aquifer.[67]

Some folks have talked about secession as if an independent Texas could be a first-world nation, up there with other dynamic, developed countries. But our politicians have allowed a billionaire from Dallas to turn a part of the state into a third-world dumping ground. In fact, three true-Texan scientists resigned from the Texas Commission on Environmental Quality rather than sign off on the nuclear dump's licensing, but their protests were like pebbles tossed into Lake Travis. They hardly made ripples, especially compared to the flood of lobbyist money that washed through Austin to seal the deal.

We're not just losing Texas in far-off, empty places, either. Right here in our own backyard, the natural gas cartel is using billions of gallons of our limited water supply to fracture the crust we live on and then injecting its toxic byproducts into disposal wells that are about as safe as the nuclear dump out past Big Spring.

There are now billboards all around town that herald the notion that the resultant natural gas harvest will last 100 years, but it's a head-scratcher for any Texans who still have brains left to scratch.

One hundred years is nothing, except in terms of human greed.

Today, Coronado wouldn't bother with Texas, and who could blame him? We're selling off our state and our state of being to the highest bidder—although that, too, is perhaps a less-acknowledged but longtime tradition in this state.

It's intensely sad.

In A Cook's Tour: Global Adventures in Extreme Cuisines, *Anthony Bourdain wrote that "Once you've been to Cambodia, you'll never stop wanting to beat Henry Kissinger to death with your bare hands." It's an empirical fact. When I visited in 2003, one in every 200 Cambodians was a victim of landmines.*

My First Epidemic
Unpublished March 22, 2020

In 2003, my friend Dan and I explored Southeast Asia. The SARS (Severe Acute Respiratory Syndrome) epidemic was winding down, but, in the last few months, a new strain had emerged, characterized by fever, diarrhea, respiratory duress and a high fatality rate. Several folks in remote Cambodian villages had succumbed to the affliction, perishing in fits of coughing, choking and delirium. Locals were sacrificing pigs and chickens and standing up straw effigies near their hut doors to ward off evil spirits

In Thailand, SARS was never mentioned. We never even saw anyone in surgical masks. We didn't realize it was still lingering in the region until we attempted to enter Cambodia. At the Poi Pet crossing station, we flashed our passports and began the visa application process. We were the only visitors in the facility.

After we paid for our visas, we were accosted by three young, machine gun-wielding representatives of a Cambodian militia. In broken English, the shortest one explained that, due to the SARS outbreak, we would be required to submit to a supervised SARS quarantine. If we coughed or sneezed or exhibited any symptoms of pneumonic complication, we would be held pending further medical examination or turned away outright. Dan looked at me and shrugged.

The quarantine staging area was simply twenty grimy, plastic lawn chairs tucked under a tarp behind the station. We dropped our backpacks and grabbed chairs. Two silent, machine gun-wielding teenagers monitored our condition.

For the duration of the quarantine, Dan and I tried to remain solemn. A couple of times Dan flashed the hint of a smile, but he wisely kept it under wraps. It's exceedingly dangerous to scoff at, laugh about or appear amused by the crude customs or processes you encounter in the Third World. Especially when your immediate point of contact has a machine gun.

On the Cambodian side of the border lay Typhoid, Hepatitis, Encephalitis, Malaria and six million land mines. It seemed ironic that the Cambodians might be concerned about two doughy Yanks bringing anything dangerous into their country. But the Vietnam war wasn't that long ago—I'm surprised they let us in at all.

When our twenty minutes were up and we had neither coughed nor sneezed or even cleared our throats, the shortest soldier returned and smiled. "Welcome to Cambodia," he said.

I experienced a strange sense of déjà vu while I was listening to a public health official on the *Texas Standard* radio show field questions regarding the Coronavirus. One annoyed caller, who claimed he saw someone who "looked sick" coughing in public, wanted to know who he should call to have them dealt with.

Toilet paper and hand-sanitizers aren't the only items flying off the shelves these days. Folks are also buying guns, and I'm afraid we're about two clicks away from pistol-packing "patriots" placing grubby lawn chairs under pop-up tents at the edge of every city limits.

149

Many white Americans argue that it's unfair—whether in regards to Affirmative Action policies, discussions of reparation for slavery, etc.—that they be held responsible or punished for the sins of their forebears. It always makes me smile, because they're apparently a little fuzzy about the first book of the Hebrew Bible and the Christian Old Testament. Adam and Eve started off in Eden, paradise, essentially a Heaven on Earth. But, because they disobeyed their creator, they were cast out, exiled, and forced to survive by the sweat or their brow, face death, etc. The punishment also applied to their descendants, who were never offered a shot at Eden the first time around. So, essentially—if the Bible is to be believed—we have all been paying for our ancestors' sins since birth. And without complaint.

The Last Man Burned at the Stake in Texas

Dissident Voice December 7, 2018

On Saturday, December 2, 1933, a 30-year-old white woman named Nellie Williams Brockman was murdered near Kountze, Texas. Brockman had headed to town to visit a department store and run into trouble along the way. She was shot to death and her body and vehicle were found partially burned. Some locals claimed they had seen a shotgun-wielding black man in the vicinity and law enforcement officials mounted an intense search for the culprit. But they turned up nothing.

A few days into the manhunt, the Kountze Police Department received a "secret" tip incriminating a young, African American ex-con named David Gregory. When Gregory, a preacher's son, became aware of the police department's suspicions, he fled to a nearby church. On December 7, Hardin County Sheriff Miles D. Jordan, and various other law enforcement personnel discovered Gregory hiding in the church's belfry. When they ordered him to come down, he refused and allegedly "flourished" a pistol (not a shotgun, the weapon the black suspect was reported carrying near the crime scene). Gregory was subsequently felled by a buckshot blast that rendered him unconscious.

Sheriff Jordan and his fellow officers transported Gregory to a Beaumont Hospital, but a portion of his neck and face were blown away. He was in critical condition and received emergency treatment, but the doctors indicated that he wouldn't survive the night.

Sheriff Jordan hoped that Gregory would regain consciousness so testimony would confirm the secret tip, but less than two hours after their arrival at the hospital, word was received that a mob had formed in Kountze and was headed towards Beaumont. Hospital authorities expressed their discomfort with harboring a suspect that could put the facility at risk and Sheriff Jordan calculated that their chances at keeping Gregory from the mob were slim, in or outside the facility.

Sheriff Jordan snuck Gregory down a back elevator, placed him in his vehicle and drove towards Vidor (seven miles east of Beaumont), planning to double-back and take Gregory to a hospital in Port Arthur (thirty miles farther south). Gregory never regained consciousness and died not long after the sheriff's car crossed into Orange County.

As the mob was still active, Sheriff Jordan was unsure of what he should do with Gregory's body. He considered a return to Beaumont unwise, so he drove to Silsbee (twenty-three miles north/northwest). At Silsbee another mob assembled and the local undertaker, fearing trouble, refused to accept Gregory's remains. With limited options and operating under the assumption that the Kountze mob was still in Beaumont, Sheriff Jordan headed back west. When he entered the Kountze community, hundreds of white men crowded in front of his vehicle. The mob seized Gregory's corpse and tied it to the back of an automobile. A fifty-car parade then dragged the body around Kountze for close to an hour, so long that a large bonfire that had been built to incinerate Gregory had burned out.

Denied a fire, the mob mutilated Gregory's body, cut out his heart and re-fastened his corpse to a car and "bounced" it through the African American section of Kountze, reportedly screaming "Nigger for breakfast!" Members of the throng then delivered the mangled corpse to the front doorstep of Gregory's mother, whom they belligerently summoned. When Mrs. Gregory appeared, however, she succinctly denied them her anticipated hysterics. She glanced over what was left of her dead son and said "You've done it right, white folks," and went back inside.

The stupefied white mob retrieved David Gregory's hide-less remains and dragged them to a new bonfire that had been built in a vacant lot not far from his home. As Gregory's body cooked, members of the mob drank coffee and ate sandwiches.

The next morning, African Americans who passed by the smoking embers were called over to "see what happened to David Gregory." Newspapers later included a photo of Gregory and his smoldering remains in their reporting.

Several years after the Gregory burning, a local white man confessed to the murder of Nellie Williams Brockman on his deathbed.

Unpleasant as it is to admit, Texas has a history of this type of monstrosity. David Gregory—like so many persons of color in America today—was denied due process, found guilty in the eyes of the mob and gunned down in a shoot-first-ask-questions-later manner that we're not unfamiliar with. He was the last known African American burned at the stake in the Lone Star state, but dozens preceded him. One in Belton, one in Temple, one in Rockwall, one in Hillsboro, one in Corsicana, one in Sherman (but two in Grayson County), one in Greensville, two in Waco, two in Tyler, three in Sulphur Springs, three in Kirvin, four in the Paris, Texas area, etc.

Gregory's cruel, forgotten fate reminds us that denial and forgetfulness are staples of white primacy and elucidates why we bristle so at threats to our historical amnesia. We white folk like to think well of ourselves, but we haven't behaved particularly well. And our shortcomings continue to prevail today.

I thought the abortion laws in Oklahoma were draconian in 2010, but the joke's on me. Eleven years after I wrote this piece, "Captain Texas" said hold my beer.

I'd Rather Have an Abortion Any Day Than Raise a Baby in Oklahoma

Dissident Voice May 12th, 2010

So, I'm a teenage girl in Oklahoma and my halfass, Bocephus boyfriend gets me pregnant. It was an accident, and I should have thought twice about letting that fool make a fool of me, telling me that he would pull it out before he came, but it's too late now. I'm preggers.

My mom and dad say I can move a trailer in next to theirs whether Bocephus marries me or not. They'll help in any way they can. But I don't want to marry that idiot. I half think he got me pregnant on purpose. And I definitely don't know if I'm ready or mature enough to bear or raise a child. I need to finish school. I probably should try to go to college.

I decide to get an abortion, but the state's new abortion laws treat me like a criminal. The Bocephuses in the Oklahoma state legislature have decided that if I want to terminate my pregnancy, I have to see an ultrasound and listen to a doctor tell me about my fetus's heart and lungs and limbs. It doesn't matter whether or not trusting a Bocephus got me into this mess. And it wouldn't matter if he raped me or was my own brother. I have to watch this video and they get to treat me like a criminal.

I've thought about it a lot and I think I've got my head around it. I think I'll go through with the abortion and then leave this crappy state, but first I have some questions.

How come Bocephus isn't being punished for lying to me? And how come he isn't required by law to sit and watch the ultrasound? He's the one who was in such a God-awful hurry. And he probably thinks he's got me right where he wants me. That scarlet letter from that book in English is still only for women. It just stands for a different word.

The Bocephuses in the state legislature may think there needs to be a law like this to make girls like me think twice before getting an abortion, but they're wrong. I get it. Pro-lifers want a woman to think about what she's doing, preventing a life or ending a life. They want me to feel a cramp of conscience, but they're wasting their time. I already do. And I already know that what I'm going to do makes me kind of like a monster in their eyes. But I ain't the only one.

Before a doctor or pro-lifer decides what I should or shouldn't do with my body, shouldn't he or she have to watch a video of an illegal, back-woods abortion? And before the Bocephuses in the state legislature decide that I have to watch footage of a fetus that's barely inside me, shouldn't they have to watch a video detailing the death and infertility rates caused by black-market abortions?

And if a young, struggling, three-quarters educated girl like me has to be held to some kind of higher standard, why shouldn't everybody be held to a higher standard?

Why don't the Bocephuses post pictures of seagulls covered in oil at every gas pump so you can see what you're doin' every time you buy gas? Why don't the Bocephuses put pictures of the Pacific Ocean Garbage Patch at the grocery checkout stands so you can see what you're contributing to every time you carry out your Pringles and Jif in plastic bags?

Do the military people who operate the Predator drones have to see pictures of bloody and maimed Afghan babies before they launch fresh attacks? Why didn't the American people get the chance to watch young Muslim men being waterboarded over and over before the Bocephuses at Fox News told them it wasn't torture?

And as we listen to coal industry bosses trying to convince us how safe coal power is, how come nobody shows actual video or pictures of black lung disease? How come smokers don't have to watch a video of what smoking does to their lungs? How come drinkers don't have to watch videos of what drinking does to their livers?

Here in America, we're all killing or dying in one way or another, and it's our God-given right. But when foolish, unwed Sooner girls try to make decisions concerning their own bodies, that's a sin.

I'd rather have an abortion any day than raise a baby in Oklahoma.

The promising members of the Legion of Doom were all clean-cut, self-important white boys. Today, they'd receive millions for legal defense funds and have to hire agents to book their conservative media appearances.

Legion of Doom-kopfs

Fort Worth Weekly April 18, 2012

OK. Tell me if this sounds familiar.

There's this group of Anglo-Americans, mostly well-to-do and some wealthy. They're not big fans of minorities (especially African-Americans) or the poor. They detest homosexuals. They feel they know better than the rest of us what's best for the community, so they've anointed themselves as the right folks to restore order and clean things up.

Republican Party 2012?

No.

Well, yes. But conservatives of the new millennium are not the ones I had in mind. I was actually thinking back to Paschal High School in Fort Worth, Texas, circa 1985. I was remembering the Legion of Doom.

By all accounts, members of Paschal High's Legion of Doom were All-American guys from good, mostly privileged families, some even inhabiting the rarefied confines of the Tanglewood and Overton Park neighborhoods on the West Side.

The Legion of Doom didn't like the growing minority population at Paschal. They didn't like the increased levels of theft and drug use that they attributed to the increased minority population at Paschal. So, based on a misguided, self-indulgent sense of righteous indignation, these clean-cut, flag-waving Caucasian students decided to do something about it.

They threatened classmates with guns and shot out a local porch light with an M-1 carbine. They vandalized lockers and used a black-painted dummy for target practice. They built a homemade bazooka and a gasoline bomb. They denigrated poor kids and homosexuals, pipe-bombed a classmate's car, and left a gutted cat splayed across another's steering wheel.

The hateful antics of the Legion, and its members' subsequent indictments and trials, were well-reported in the 1980s. But what didn't get much coverage were the Legion's philosophical underpinnings. Members of the Legion were conservative athletes and honor students. They were strait-laced sons of lawyers and executives and even one Christian minister. As one member's mother put it, they were all "pro-Republican."

And the relevance of the Legion of Doom's political leanings should never be downplayed.

The Ronald Reagan presidency ushered in an alarming uptick in all things conservative, and many Republicans—especially those who had hung their heads in shame since Watergate—were fat and sassy again. As pop act Huey Lewis and the News so aptly phrased things, it was once again "hip to be square."

But the Legion obviously took things too far. Their victims had had a hard enough time trying to act white or straight or upper-middle class; demanding that they be square or else just added insult to the many injuries the Legion inflicted.

All these years later, of course, it simply seems that the Legion of Doom was just ahead of its time.

In a society where abortion providers are gunned down in church, politicians are shot in public, and African-American teenagers are killed for being black, the Legion of Doom today almost seems tame. They might even be a hit with hardcore Republicans and would undoubtedly be hailed by blowhards like Rush Limbaugh as good, misunderstood Americans (like him).

We live in troubling times. It seems that for every sane person you run into, you meet two wackos. And not Charles Manson or Jeffrey Dahmer wackos. I'm referring to Ward and June Cleaver wackos. I'm talking about Mayberry freaks. A large percentage of Middle America appears to have gone zombie and can only be sated by gorging on hatred and fear.

In the 1980s, a sociology professor from Texas Christian University noted that Legion members' self-image as well-meaning vigilantes working to rid their community of destructive elements smacked of a rationalization "to soothe their conscience."

Smells like team spirit in the trenches of the 2012 Republican base.

A black man is president. Women's reproductive rights have strengthened their independence. Gays are allowed to fight for their country. The nation is becoming more open-minded and diverse.

In places like Arizona, Virginia, and Texas, the right is pushing back, encouraging voter disenfranchisement efforts, trans-vaginal intimidation, etc. Another legion is overstepping its bounds.

When will we fight back?

Paraphrasing Oliver Hazard Perry, commander of the American fleet at the Battle of Lake Erie in 1813, we have met the enemy, and he is us.

UFO U-Turn

Fort Worth Weekly January 30, 2008

Before *Close Encounters of the Third Kind* came out in 1977, Steven Spielberg & Co. sponsored an art contest for kids across the country. The goal was to submit a rendering that most closely resembled the space aliens that would be featured in the movie. Like thousands of kids around the country, I answered the challenge. Sci-fi was right up my alley.

I didn't win. In fact, I never even got a response. When the movie came out and I saw the aliens at the end, I felt cheated. They didn't seem anything like the space creatures I'd seen in other sci-fi flicks and comic books—they weren't even wearing space suits.

When a UFO recently appeared right down Hwy. 377 in Stephenville, it reminded me of my early fascination with space aliens, and, sitting two counties away (as terrestrial objects fly), I was a little jealous. Watching movie stars see aliens or UFOs for the first time is not quite as exciting as seeing the genuine article yourself.

I had read and re-read *Chariots of the Gods* when I was a kid and watched the X-Files for years. I knew the truth was out there—but I'd never thought to look in Stephenville. I should have—Texas seems prime territory for visits from E.T.'s kinfolks.

The first documented visit to North Texas by space types was also a rural jaunt, 111 years ago in a town called Aurora. It's right off State Hwy. 114, just southeast of Boyd. As the story goes, a slow-moving UFO appeared in the sky around dawn and crashed into the town judge's windmill, the explosion destroying the windmill, the attached water tank, and the judge's flower garden. Aurora residents found a small, charbroiled alien in the debris and gave him a proper burial in the local cemetery.

The second space visit to our area came fifty years later. The "flying disc" that reportedly crashed near Roswell, N. M., in 1947 was transported to the Fort Worth Army Airfield (formerly Carswell, now the Naval Air Station Joint Reserve Base) for further examination, on orders of Gen. Roger M. Ramey, commander of the Eighth Air Force. The military had already initiated a spin campaign in New Mexico suggesting that the mysterious disc and its otherworldly occupants had actually been a fallen weather balloon, and when the object and its dead crew arrived at the airfield, officials quickly confirmed that report. Unofficially, Ramey successfully swept the real story under the rug, and more dead aliens experienced North Texas D.O.A.

So far there have been no extraterrestrial casualties associated with the Stephenville visit—the third time around appears to be the proverbial charm. Their massive spacecraft was visible for several moments on January 8th, and dozens of local residents, including a pilot and a constable, got a good look at the surreal deal.

Now, local car dealers are accepting UFOs as trade-ins, city secretaries are wearing green alien masks, and high school students are going to class wearing tin foil on their heads.

Lost in the spectacle, however, is one alarming note: While we got a good look at them (or at least their spaceship), they got a good look at us. And I bet they felt cheated. If I had traveled hundreds of light-years in search of new life forms on another planet, and they turned out to be as shabby, ignorant, and greedy as we are, I'd be pretty demoralized.

We're fat and lazy. Our lives lack meaning and a real sense of purpose. We have very little compassion for those less fortunate than us. We don't believe in sharing things or working together. We can't live in harmony with our environment or the hapless thousands of other species with which we share our planet.

More of us believe in the Easter Bunny than in evolution, and even though danger and self-destruction lurk behind each page-flip of the calendar, we seem incapable of disciplined political, economic, and social imperatives. As a result, we have so much internal self-contempt that we enjoy watching *American Idol*, *Jackass*, and *Borat*, just to see folks exactly like us being abused, degraded, and humiliated.

I say, let's enjoy our extraterrestrial guests while we can because, after we finish building stupid, pointless border walls to keep earthly "aliens" out, we'll probably start building retractable-roofed domes over our cities to keep space aliens out.

In fact, if a spaceship full of curious beings from some other planet swooped down and attempted to make contact with me, I'd advise them to high-tentacle it back to wherever they came from, before some slick operator here figures out how to trace back their route, strip-mine their planet, and start selling the inhabitants boxed sets of *Survivor* reruns.

I was trying to be sarcastic when I penned this ten years ago, but I'm afraid "Captain Texas" mistook it for an action plan and pinned it under the "To Do" section of his bulletin board.

Gun Bless America
Unpublished April 19, 2011

Oh boy, here we go again.

On April 21st, a Houston kindergartner carried a gun into an elementary school, and it fired when he was trying to pull it out and show it off at lunch. There's no mystery regarding what happened next. The peace-mongers had a hissy-fit.

One six-year-old has a shooting accident, the discharge of which barely scratches two of his classmates and hardly harms him and the gun control patrol pounces on firearm advocates as if they're defenseless worms.

The peace-mongers are absurdly predictable. You can almost set your watch according to their paranoia.

The spread of gun freedoms make the gun control patrol nervous, so they look for any reason just to limit our Second Amendment rights. Now they're even talking about putting metal detectors at elementary school entries . . . as if we couldn't dream up better ways to waste of the tax-payers' money.

Well, I've got bad news for the "Love Thine Enemy" crowd. If Gabrielle Giffords had been carrying a gun at the Casas Adobes Safeway supermarket parking lot on January 8th, maybe she could have pulled it out and shot Jared Lee Loughner before he shot her in the head. And Christina Taylor Green, the little 9-year-old who was shot in the face—if she'd have been prepared like the 6-year-old who brought a gun to his Houston elementary school in April, she could have defended herself.

Has anyone ever considered the possibility that the kid who brought the gun to school just wanted to exercise his God-given, Constitutionally-established right to protect himself? Is it possible he was tired of being bullied?

A few weeks back, President Obama lectured us all about bullying. Problem solved.

If all the kids in all the schools carried guns, there wouldn't be any bullying. And teachers—well they're just another branch of the government and Lord knows we have to protect ourselves from the government.

Keeping handguns out of elementary schools is just another example of Liberals trying take away our freedoms, deny our rights and legislate the sissy song of naïve peace-mongers.

Here in Texas, good, patriotic Americans like Governor Rick Perry are making it easier to vote if you're white and own a gun. At least he knows who should be at the front of the line.

In Florida, good, patriotic Americans like Governor Rick Scott are actually having to pass a bill to keep Sunshine state gun-owners from being harassed by pediatricians, who routinely assail them with intrusive, judgmental questions like "Do you own a gun?" and "Are you keeping it stored properly?"

Since when did foot doctors start working in cahoots with the Bureau of Alcohol, Tobacco and Firearms?

I, for one, am not going to stand for it. My kids will make me a grandparent someday, and I'm going to insist my grandchildren be allowed to carry firearms to their elementary schools if they want and I'll even take it a step further. I'm going to design and market a baby bottle that's shaped like a pistol, with the barrel end comprising an

163

inflexible nipple; instead of sucking, our babies can just pull the trigger. It will limit their oral fixation and increase their manual dexterity. They'll be aiming before they can read and maiming before they can walk. They'll be gun-toters instead of gum-flappers.

It's time to stand up to the peace-mongers. There's no use in sheltering our kids. The world is a dangerous place and we don't want them showing up to a pillow fight with a pop-gun. Might as well get them used to the real thing. Might as well prepare our children for their civic duty.

Freedom isn't free. And neither is self-delusion.

If the gun control patrol wants my guns, they'll have to pry them from the gums of my precious, swaddled grandbabies.

Gun Bless . . . *I mean God Bless* . . . America.

Who is that masked man? Is "Captain Texas" really Snidely Whiplash in disguise?

Snidely Abbott
Fort Worth Weekly July 28, 2021

On Thursday, June 24, 2021, leaders of several indigenous groups in Canada announced that investigators utilizing ground-penetrating radar had located the bodies of at least six hundred children in unmarked graves on the site of the former Marieval Indian Residential School about eighty-five miles east of Regina, the capital of Saskatchewan.

The news and the numbers were staggering, and Canadian Prime Minister Justin Trudeau tweeted that he was "terribly saddened" to hear about the discovery, and that "we will tell the truth about these injustices." Saskatchewan Premier Scott Moe added that the entire citizenry of Saskatchewan mourned the discovery of the unmarked graves.

Now, first, for all my fellow products of the Texas education system, a Canadian prime minister is sort of like an American president. Think of President Biden as a fossilized version of Trudeau.

Second, a Canadian premier is sort of like an American governor. So think of Greg Abbott as a vapid, wheelchair-bound version of Moe.

Granted, neither Trudeau nor Moe are ideal Dudley Do-Right material, but that's okay. Biden is no Dudley Do-Right himself, and Abbott is no Lone Ranger. Oh, and Saskatchewan is not where bigfoot or sasquatches live.

So, six hundred dead indigenous children and not only are Trudeau and Moe talking about it, but they're expressing remorse and Trudeau is pledging to get to the bottom of it.

Is there something in the water in the Great White North?

Here in the Not-So-Great Lone Star South, our "premiers" are not "terribly saddened" by news of unmarked mass graves, especially if they are full of indigenous bodies or the descendants of slaves. And they have no interest in telling the truth about injustices, much less allowing the truth to be taught in our schools.

The Slocum Massacre is an excellent example.

The Marieval Indian Residential School, which operated from 1899 to 1997, was run by Catholic nuns and the students lived on-site. Most of the graves had gravestones originally, but they were removed by Catholic officials. This is a travesty and an injustice, no question. As is forcing indigenous children to leave their families to attend white Christian schools. But the Texas version is arguably worse.

In the Slocum area of Southeastern Anderson County, there are also unmarked graves that contain the final resting places of hundreds of victims.

Unmarked mass graves.

Unmarked mass graves where the bodies of innocent men, women and children are piled up like animals in a perpetual state of unrest. They never had individual resting places, much less their own headstones. And did I mention that one of the mass graves is also located at a school?

At the Marieval Indian Residential School in the Saskatchewan province of Canada, the bodies in unmarked graves were interred over a number of decades. At the Silver Creek School playground in the southeastern corner of Anderson County (right off County Road

1208) in Texas, the bodies in an unmarked mass grave were dumped there over a long weekend. A long weekend of white slaughter and bloodshed.

The bodies of the indigenous schoolchildren in Saskatchewan were apparently interred in a designated area, originally marked with headstones. The bodies of the men, women and children who died in the Silver Creek section of the Slocum area, were buried in a large pit under the Silver Creek School playground—because the grass and dirt above a playground is always disturbed, and the perpetrators of the Slocum Massacre knew that Texas Rangers looking for victims of the atrocity would be a lot less suspicious of disturbed earth at a playground than anywhere else.

A few years back, George Avery, director of the anthropology/archaeology lab at Stephen F. Austin University, offered to run his department's ground-penetrating radar equipment over the area that Silver Creek School playground formerly sat, but the white owner of the land refused to allow descendants of the victims of the Slocum Massacre (or George Avery) access. And when confronted by Constance Hollie-Jawaid, the chief spokesperson for descendants of the victims of Slocum Massacre, the white owner bragged that there were up to fifty bodies located under the former playground, but they belonged to him because they were on his land. He said the bodies were his "property" and there was nothing Hollie-Jawaid could do about it.

Now, I realize Greg Abbott is no Dudley Do-Right. But Hollie-Jawaid and many of the descendants of Slocum Massacre victims are his constituents. And the Texas state legislature did pass a House Resolution acknowledging the Slocum Massacre in 2011. And Hollie-Jawaid did compel the Texas Historical Commission to approve a historical marker commemorating the Slocum Massacre in 2015 and have it placed and dedicated in the Slocum area in early 2016. And, hell, a few weeks back, Forest Gump mentioned the Slocum Massacre in a *New York Times* editorial!

How come Greg Abbott has never mentioned the Slocum Massacre?

How come Greg Abbott hasn't inquired about the unmarked mass graves in the Slocum area or ordered an official investigation?

How come our governor behaves more like a Snidely Whiplash than a Dudley Do-Right?

No, that's not a type-o.

$th of July

Dissident Voice July 12, 2012

Four years ago this month, a University of Minnesota student named Max P. Sanders was charged with bribery for putting his presidential vote up for sale on eBay.

That preceding May, Sanders had set a minimum bid of $10 for his presidential pick and offered to furnish photographic evidence of his eBay-bought choice in the voting booth. "Good luck!" he said in the listing. "Your country depends on You!"

The auction was something of a lark, of course, and Sanders received no offers. But the prank caught the attention of the Minnesota Secretary of State's office and Hennepin County prosecutors were alerted. On July 3, 2008, Sanders was charged with one felony count of bribery under an 1893 state law that makes it a crime to offer to buy or sell a vote.

John Aiken, a spokesman for the Minnesota Secretary of State's office said "There are people that have died for this country for our right to vote, and, to take something that lightly, to say, 'I can be bought'—it's a real shame."

The Hennepin County attorney on the case, Mike Freeman, concurred. "A lot of us served in the military trying to protect the right to vote," he said. "This is serious stuff."

Well, yes. And no.

Mostly no. I'm sure many of you had as hard a time keeping a straight face reading this as I did writing it.

Bribery? Sold suffrage?

Has anybody been paying attention to Capitol Hill lately?

Corporate lobbyists spend hundreds of millions of dollars a year bribing our congressional representatives to cast votes that support heinous corporate indulgences and secure preposterous levels of corporate immunity. Billionaires spend hundreds of millions of dollars a year propping up puppet politicians to lick their boots in exchange for bottomless campaign coffers and cushy seats on corporate boards in their political afterlives. And our Supreme Court—via its Citizen's United decision—now enjoys its lowest approval rating ever for not just enabling the wholesale financial confiscation of our political system, but actually sanctifying it.

Does the inescapable reality of our representative democracy being bought and sold every day really have to be pointed out? Don't most of us simply accept it now and expect it?

To be fair, the charges that came down against Sanders the day before the 4th of July in 2008 obviously smacked of an attempt at political point-scoring. But I can't help but go back to Aiken and Freeman's ridiculous indignation.

Does anyone really believe that the brave men and women Aiken and Freeman referred to fought for or sacrificed their lives for a nation where multinational corporate personhood holds more sway in the election booths than real, live, flesh and blood American citizens?

Does anybody honestly believe our soldiers knowingly and voluntarily risk their lives so our elections can be bought and sold by shadowy Capitalist entities?

The U. S. Supreme Court's Citizen's United decision[68] basically declared money a form of free speech and enabled corporations and billionaires to anonymously (and therefore freely) purchase political offices and pay for their say in our governance.

To some extent things may have always been thus, but now they're thusly so one hundred or one thousand fold.

We *can* be bought.

Our lives can be dictated by any frat-boy heir with a trust fund or three to spare.

So when you take a seat in a local ballpark or fold out a lawn chair near a public space to watch the community Fourth of July fireworks show, please ruminate a bit before the pyrotechnics start.

Yesterday, our flag wasn't emblazoned with a C-note. Yesterday, our real allegiance wasn't pledged to a stack of grubby cash.

Today we are one nation, under dollar signs, with liberty and justice for those who can afford it.

Our country no longer belongs to us, and it certainly no longer depends on us to be anything other than gullible, over-consuming, semi-sentient dupes.

Do we still live in a place where the right to vote is really worth fighting or dying for?

Donald J. Trump may have been a damn sight worse than George W. Bush, but we don't have to claim Trump.

Proud Again?

Fort Worth Weekly October 17, 2007

A couple of months ago, I vacationed in Colorado. I loved the drive from Fort Worth to Denver. Leaving Cowtown, the sky gets expansive, anchored only by rolling prairies.

Things flatten out for a while in the Panhandle, but the landscape begins to ripple again in New Mexico, and by the time you reach I-25 in Colorado, the Rockies are beside you, and you skirt them the rest of the way. It's a great road trip, the kind of journey that allows you to turn everything off for a while. You forget about the ways you're prostituting yourself at work and compromising your principles to get by. You even quit worrying about the idiots who are running this country.

That part of the relaxation ended before I got back to Fort Worth, however. It was over as soon as I crossed back into Texas. During the first world war of the 20th century, an American radical named Randolph Bourne said that the purpose of education was to prepare folks to recognize a revolution. Not just when it's happening, but also when it needs to happen. It seems to me that the purpose of a vacation is to give us the space in which to remember who we are and who we should be, day in and day out. A journey allows us to step outside our usual rituals and routines, where we can ad lib.

On the way back, I'd come in on Hwy. 87, cruising through the Kiowa National Grassland. I'd just left Clayton, N.M., daydreaming through sunny grasslands on the way to Dalhart. But my respite with the existential sublime ended at the small town of Texline, so dubbed because it sits on the Texas-New Mexico border. At the town's edge sat a "Welcome To Texas" sign featuring a large Texas flag. So far, so good. But at the bottom, under a brief entreaty to motorists to drive friendly ("the Texas way"), there was an addendum: "Proud Home of George W. Bush."

I almost turned around.

I started thinking about how un-proud of George W. I am and shrinking at the thought of the number of state-line signs on which this inanity must be posted. With a nation that has been reduced to a polarized, paralyzed wreck, how can we embrace the demolition man? The citizens of New Orleans don't claim former FEMA director Michael Brown. The swindled Native American Indian tribes don't claim Jack Abramoff.[69] And Valerie Plame certainly doesn't profess unwavering respect and admiration for Scooter Libby[70] or Dick Cheney.

Then I thought, let's get beyond Bush and his tribe (And thank goodness we'll be beyond him as a nation in a few months. Have you seen the pins and posters and little clocks that count down the time left in his administration?) We have to think about what we're going to do when this dim and shameful chapter in our history is over.

The last seven years have been an education—a painful, scarring education—and if they've taught us anything, they've taught us it's time for a change. A drastic change.

A revolution.

It won't require guns or a militia. It won't require lopping off any heads (although a few could probably use it). All it will require is courage, faith, and perseverance. Courage to challenge the laziness and complacency that damn us to our current, destructive paths. Faith to believe that something better can be accomplished. Perseverance to commit to the difficult road ahead.

Right now, in the United States—and indeed in Texas—our government doesn't want us to ask questions, our corporate lords don't want us to think for ourselves, and our political leaders don't want us to challenge the status quo. They prefer an ignorant, easily manipulated electorate. An electorate that falls for whisper campaigns and rigged town-meeting formats. One that is suckered by staged photo ops and rhetorical grandstanding.

But it's not as simple as changing horses. We need a vacation from the two-party system altogether. The Republican and Democratic parties are two sides of the same tired coin. As long as the frontrunners from either party are sons or wives of former presidents, as long as they're taking their marching orders from the same money piles as their predecessors, the coin is no longer worth flipping.

It's time for a change. We need to get their attention. If our current and potential political representatives are not worried, nothing will change. And our shames will multiply.

*The twilight of the idles (apologies to Friedrich Wilhelm Nietzsche[71]
for riffing on his title)[72] was already beginning its approach in 2011.
How much time is left?*

Twilight of the Idles

Dissident Voice December 18th, 2010

The 112th session of the United States Congress doesn't convene until January, but the GOP is already flexing its ignorance.

Last week Republicans announced they would be scrapping the four-year-old Select Committee for Energy Independence and Global Warming because it was created by the Democrats to promote "job-killing national energy taxes," and they wanted to save taxpayers money by reducing frivolous expenditures. They relayed this folly with deadpan earnestness, as if it was their solemn duty to be purposefully obtuse; as if it were part of their party platform, a matter of principle or impassioned lack thereof. And, of course, that's exactly what it was.

For all the weeping and gnashing of teeth they cued up for the cameras regarding the economic trials and tribulations we'll be passing on to our great-grandkids through deficit spending, they are voluntarily heedless of the ecological calamities our descendants will inherit due to idle dithering.

I realize this Democrat-created committee probably amounted to little more than a token gesture towards the cause, but at least it acknowledged global warming and our untenable reliance on fossil fuels. At least it placed these issues in direct proximity with our legislative process, whereby they might accidentally slip into serious legislative discussions by osmosis (if nothing else). This committee was a step, however infantile.

The GOP and most of its supporters keep squealing about the costs of being environmentally conscious and crying about insufficient evidence regarding climate change, but exorbitant costs and lack of evidence didn't stop them from invading Iraq. Remember the one percent doctrine?

Also known as the "Cheney Doctrine," it stipulated that if there was one percent chance Iraq was working on nuclear weapons, we had to treat it as a certainty in terms of response. It basically gave the Bush Administration carte blanche to invade Iraq if a yellowing Nuclear Valdez cassette tape was found in Baghdad.

There's clearly more than a one percent chance that human beings are accelerating or exacerbating the conditions responsible for global warming, and these conditions will probably lead to catastrophes that make the threat of nukes in Iraq or the deficit spending that occurred during the Great Recession look as profound and menacing as the flutter of Bristol Palin's[73] right eyelid. Where's the prudence, the caution, the weepy, teeth-gnashing humanity? Is it only reserved for scare tactics?

So be it. Here's something scary.

The twilight of the idles is approaching. Our parents and grandparents had the luxury of growing up in a time when the fact that we were imperiling our environment was not widely known or understood. Most of us would love to have been afforded that sense of existential innocence, but it's impossible to recapture. We're running Eden into the ground. We can no longer ignore the fact that our natural resources are finite, our habitats are fragile and our ecosystems are delicately balanced. We aren't going to be able to live as recklessly as previous generations did.

If we ignore the preponderance of evidence regarding climate change and the implications that global warming portends, the last thing our descendants will have to worry about is dealing with the federal deficit. They'll simply be trying to survive.

There's no reason to sugar-coat things. At our present rate of consumption, waste and resource degradation, we're only a century away from a self-induced, ecological holocaust. And the point of no return may very well be reached in our lifetime.

We need to start using less and wanting less. Extravagance needs to invite scorn and shame, not envy. Rapid, incessantly rising profit margins need to begin to be treated like unsustainably high blood pressure, not a healthy pulse. We need to limit population growth, preserve our natural ecosystems, invest in renewable energy sources, detoxify our rivers, streams and water sources, ban industrial fishing, eradicate industrial farming, eliminate corporate personhood, restrain corporate multi-nationalism, dismantle our for-profit military-industrial complex, etc., etc.

You can't pretend to care about the quality of life for our great-grandchildren if you're unwilling to address global warming. You can't claim to care about the future of this country if you're not committed to steering it toward cleaner power sources.

A revolution in thinking must be achieved. We must replace fossil fuels. We must learn that less is more. We must re-learn how to live in harmony with nature.

Materialism must face the guillotine. Capitalism must be pilloried. If the United States does not lead, or at least join, this revolution, it will likely go the way of the USSR. And rightfully so.

The clock is ticking.

NOTES

[1] Joe Barton (born September 15, 1949) is an American politician who represented Texas's 6th congressional district in the U.S. House of Representatives from 1985 to 2019. The district included Arlington, part of Fort Worth, and several small towns and rural areas south of the Dallas–Fort Worth Metroplex. In 2010, Barton defended BP in hearings regarding the 2008 Deepwater Horizon oil spill in the Gulf of Mexico. He was a steadfast climate change denier and a staunch opponent of abortion and LGBTQ rights. In 2017, Barton announced he would not seek reelection in 2018 after sexually explicit photos that he had shared with multiple women surfaced online.

[2] On May 27, 1995, British actor Hugh Grant was arrested for receiving oral sex from a prostitute in his car on Hollywood's Sunset Boulevard. The story attracted an inordinate amount of attention, even in the tabloids.

[3] "Bartleby, the Scrivener: A Story of Wall Street" is a short story by American writer Herman Melville, first serialized anonymously in two parts in the November and December 1853 issues of *Putnam's Magazine* and later reprinted with minor textual alterations in his *The Piazza Tales* in 1856. In the story, a Wall Street lawyer hires a new clerk who, though initially hard-working, eventually begins to refuse to perform even the most menial of tasks. When the perplexed lawyer begins to press Bartleby on the matter, repeatedly demanding he perform this task or that, the clerk's response is always the same: "I would prefer not to."

[4] On February 19, 1982, a drunken Ozzy urinated on San Antonio's sacred 60-foot-high, 1939 Cenotaph, a monument erected at the Alamo Plaza (located directly across from the Alamo building) to honor the dead.

The San Antonio Police arrested Ozzy, and he spent part of the afternoon in a local jail on charges of public intoxication. He was released later that evening on $40 bond and performed at the city's Hemisfair Arena Convention Center. Osbourne was subsequently banned from playing in San Antonio again until 1992, when he formally apologized to the city and donated $10,000 to the Daughters of the Republic of Texas.

[5] When rock star Phil Collins saw the Disney production of *Davy Crockett, King of the Wild Frontier* as a child, he became enthralled by the story of the Alamo. After achieving rock and roll stardom as a member of Genesis, he began collecting Alamo artifacts, eventually amassing one of the most extensive (and expensive) Alamo collections in the world. In 2014, Collins donated over 400 pieces from his collection to the Texas General Land Office, the agency that oversees the Alamo.

[6] James Mercer Langston Hughes (February 1, 1901 – May 22, 1967) was an American poet, social activist, novelist, playwright, and columnist from Joplin,

Missouri. One of the earliest innovators of the literary art form called jazz poetry, Hughes is most remembered for being a leader of the Harlem Renaissance.

[7] Eric Arthur Blair (June 25, 1903 – January 21, 1950)—known by his *nom de plume*, George Orwell, was a brilliant English novelist, essayist, journalist and critic. His writing is characterized by lucid prose, biting social criticism and opposition to totalitarianism. He is the author of *Animal Farm* (1945), *1984* (1949), and *Homage to Catalonia* (1938). Orwell's work remains remarkably relevant and influential in popular culture and political culture, and the adjective "Orwellian"—describing totalitarian and authoritarian social practices—is now part of the English language.

[8] Paul Leroy Robeson (April 9, 1898 – January 23, 1976) was an American bass baritone concert artist and stage and film actor who became famous for his cultural accomplishments and his political activism. Educated at Rutgers College and Columbia University, his political activities began with his involvement with unemployed workers and anti-imperialist students whom he met in Britain and his opposition to fascism which led to his support for the Republican cause in the Spanish Civil War. He later became active in the civil rights movement and other social justice campaigns in the United States. His criticism of the United States government and its foreign policies got him blacklisted during the McCarthy era.

[9] Federico del Sagrado Corazón de Jesús García Lorca (June 5, 1898 – August 19, 1936) was a beloved Spanish poet, playwright, and theatre director. He was executed by Nationalist forces at the beginning of the Spanish Civil War, and his remains have never been located.

[10] Ricardo Eliécer Neftalí Reyes Basoalto (July 12, 1904 – September 23, 1973)—better known as Pablo Neruda—was a Chilean poet-diplomat and politician who won the Nobel Prize for Literature in 1971.

[11] Georges André Malraux (November 3, 1901 – November 23, 1976) was a French novelist and art theorist, later serving as the minister of cultural affairs of France. His novel *La Condition Humaine* (Man's Fate, 1933) won the Prix Goncourt.

[12] Ambrose Gwinnett Bierce (June 24, 1842 – circa 1914) was an American short story writer, journalist, poet, and Civil War veteran. A prolific and versatile wordsmith, Bierce was regarded as one of the most influential journalists in the United States and a pioneer of realist fiction. His book *The Devil's Dictionary* was named one of "The 100 Greatest Masterpieces of American Literature" by the American Revolution Bicentennial Administration, and his story "An Occurrence at Owl Creek Bridge" is considered one of the most well-known and frequently anthologized tales in American letters.

[13] William Henry Gates III (born October 28, 1955) is an American, multibillionaire business magnate, software developer, investor, author, and philanthropist. He was the co-founder of Microsoft Corporation, alongside his late childhood friend Paul Allen. During his career at Microsoft, Gates held the positions of chairman,

CEO, president and chief software architect, while also being the largest individual shareholder until May 2014.

[14] Gary Arlen Kildall (May 19, 1942 – July 11, 1994) was an American computer scientist and microcomputer entrepreneur.

[15] Glenn Lee Beck (born February 10, 1964) is a conservative political commentator, conspiracy theorist, radio host, and television producer. He is the CEO, founder, and owner of Mercury Radio Arts, the parent company of his television and radio network TheBlaze. He hosts the Glenn Beck Radio Program, a popular talk-radio show nationally syndicated on Premiere Radio Networks.

[16] Rush Hudson Limbaugh III (January 12, 1951 – February 17, 2021) was an American radio personality, conservative political commentator and television show personality. He was best known as the host of *The Rush Limbaugh Show*, which was nationally syndicated on AM and FM radio stations. Limbaugh became one of the premier conservative voices in the United States during the 1990s and hosted a national television show from 1992 to 1996. He was among the most highly compensated figures in American radio history; in 2018 Forbes listed his earnings at $84.5 million.

[17] Marian Keech's real name was Dorothy Martin (1900–1992). She was a Chicago prophet and one of the subjects of the book *When Prophecy Fails* (1956).

[18] During the early stages of the Iraq War, members of the United States Military and the CIA committed a number of human rights violations and war crimes against detainees in the Abu Ghraib prison in Iraq under the direct orders of the Secretary of Defense, Donald Rumsfeld. These criminal acts included physical abuse, torture, rape, sodomy, and murder. The crimes came to light after the publication of photographs of the abuse by *CBS News* in April 2004.

[19] The Plame affair (also known as the "CIA Leak Scandal" and "Plamegate") was a political scandal that revolved around journalist Robert Novak's public identification of Valerie Plame as a covert operative for the CIA in 2003. The leak originated in the George W. Bush White House as a form of retaliation. After President Bush stated that "Saddam Hussein recently sought significant quantities of uranium from Africa" during the run-up to the 2003 invasion of Iraq, Wilson published an editorial implying that the Bush Administration's uranium claims were frivolous in a July 2003 edition of *The New York Times*.

[20] Katie Couric (born January 7, 1957) is an American television and online journalist, presenter, producer, and author. Couric has been a television host at all of the Big Three television networks in the United States. She worked for NBC News from 1989 to 2006, *CBS News* from 2006 to 2011 and she was Yahoo's Global News Anchor from 2013 to 2017.

[21] Erich Maria Remarque (June 22, 1898 – September 25, 1970) was a German novelist. His landmark novel *All Quiet on the Western Front* (1928), about the

German military experience of World War I, was an international best-seller and was subsequently adapted into a film of the same name in 1930.

[22] Salvador Guillermo Allende (June 26, 1908 – September 11, 1973) was a Chilean physician and socialist politician who served as the president of Chile from November 3, 1970 until his death on September 11, 1973. As president, Allende sought to nationalize major industries, expand education and improve the living standards for working class Chileans. He clashed with the right-wing parties that controlled Congress and with the judiciary.

On September 11, 1973, the military moved to oust Allende in a coup d'état supported by the United States Central Intelligence Agency.

[23] Juan Jacobo Árbenz Guzmán (September 14, 1913 – January 27, 1971) was a Guatemalan military officer and politician who served as the 25th President of Guatemala. He was Minister of National Defense from 1944 to 1951, and the second democratically elected President of Guatemala, from 1951 to 1954. He was a major figure in the ten-year Guatemalan Revolution, which represented some of the few years of representative democracy in Guatemalan history.

Árbenz's progressive policies angered the United Fruit Company, which lobbied the United States government to have him removed. Under the questionable pretense that the United States was seriously concerned about the presence of communists in the Guatemalan government, Árbenz was ousted in the 1954 Guatemalan coup d'état engineered by the U.S. Department of State and the CIA. In October 2011, the Guatemalan government issued an apology for Árbenz's overthrow.

[24] Francis Augustus Hamer (March 17, 1884 – July 10, 1955) was a Texas Ranger who led the 1934 posse that tracked down and killed criminals Bonnie Parker and Clyde Barrow. Renowned for his toughness, marksmanship and investigative skill, he acquired status in the Southwest as the archetypal Texas Ranger.

[25] In terms of the media coverage of George W. Bush during his presidency, it is arguably a professional courtesy that he was characterized as simply being "incurious" rather pronounced ignorant, obtuse or idiotic.

[26] Florida emerged as the key state in the 2000 presidential campaign. On election night, it became clear that whoever won the Sunshine State would be president. Bush held an extremely narrow lead in the vote by the end of election night, triggering an automatic recount. The Florida Supreme Court ordered a partial manual recount, but the U. S. Supreme Court stepped in and ordered an end to this process, leaving Bush with a victory in both the state and the national election.

[27] William Daniel Cunningham (born December 11, 1947) is a Conservative radio and television talk show host, commentator, attorney, and entrepreneur. He has been named "one of the most prolific purveyors of hate speech" by *Media Matters*.

[28] Pussy Riot is a Russian feminist protest punk rock and performance art group based in Moscow. Founded in August 2011, it has had a revolving membership of approximately eleven women. The group has staged unauthorized provocative guerrilla performances in public places, and the performances were filmed as music videos and posted on the Internet. Pussy Riot's lyrical themes included feminism, LGBT rights and opposition to Russian President Vladimir Putin and his policies.

[29] The Chernobyl disaster was a nuclear accident that occurred on Saturday, April 26, 1986, at the No. 4 reactor at the Chernobyl Nuclear Power Plant, near the city of Pripyat in the north of the Ukrainian SSR in the Soviet Union. It is considered the worst nuclear disaster in human history both in terms of cost and casualties, and is one of only two nuclear accidents rated at seven (the maximum severity) on the International Nuclear Event Scale, the other being the Fukushima Daiichi nuclear disaster in Japan in 2011.

[30] John Calvin Thomas (born 2 December 1942) is an American syndicated columnist, pundit, writer and radio commentator.

[31] Don Erler was a contributing columnist to the *Fort Worth Star-Telegram* and a Texas businessman.

[32] Daisy Joe is the Director/Coordinator for the Black Citizens for Justice Law & Order, a non-profit civil rights organization that was founded in 1969 to provide a bastion of strength and unity to those who perceive they've been racially abused.

[33] Margaret Eleanor Atwood (born November 18, 1939) is a Canadian poet, novelist, literary critic, essayist, teacher, environmental activist, and inventor. Since 1961, she has published eighteen books of poetry, eighteen novels, eleven books of non-fiction, nine collections of short fiction, eight children's books, and two graphic novels. Her work has garnered numerous awards and honors, including two Booker Prizes, the Arthur C. Clarke Award, the Governor General's Award, the Franz Kafka Prize, Princess of Asturias Awards and the National Book Critics and PEN Center USA Lifetime Achievement Awards.[2] A number of her works, most notably *The Handmaid's Tale*, have been adapted for film and television.

[34] Jason Nelson Robards Jr. (July 26, 1922 – December 26, 2000) was an American actor who received two Academy Awards, a Tony Award, a Primetime Emmy Award, and the Cannes Film Festival Award for Best Actor.

[35] Sir Ridley Scott (born November 30, 1937) is an English film director and producer. He directed the science fiction horror film *Alien* (1979), the neo-noir dystopian film *Blade Runner* (1982), the road adventure *Thelma & Louise* (1991), the historical drama *Gladiator* (2000), and the science fiction film *The Martian* (2015).

[36] Born in California and raised in Texas, Mary Tyler "Molly" Ivins (August 30, 1944 – January 31, 2007) was a much-admired American newspaper columnist, author, political commentator and humorist.

[37] The colloquial name of former Governor Rick Perry's hunting ranch.

[38] Christine Therese O'Donnell (born August 27, 1969) is an American conservative activist in the Tea Party movement best known for her 2010 campaign for the United States Senate seat (of Delaware) vacated by Joe Biden.

[39] Sharron Elaine Angle (born July 26, 1949) is an American politician who served as a Republican member of the Nevada Assembly from 1999 to 2007. In 2010, she ran unsuccessfully as the Republican nominee for the U.S. Senate seat in Nevada, garnering 45 percent of the vote. In January of 2011, Congressman Jim Clyburn said that "Sharron Angle's endorsement of 'Second Amendment remedies' in her losing Nevada campaign against Senate Majority Leader Harry Reid contributed to the shooting of Rep. Gabby Giffords."

[40] Sarah Louise Palin (born February 11, 1964) is an American politician, commentator and reality television personality who served as the governor of Alaska from 2006 until her resignation in 2009. In 2008, she was the first female Republican vice presidential nominee alongside Arizona Senator John McCain. The McCain-Palin ticket lost the 2008 election to Barack Obama and Joe Biden.

[41] George Richard Tiller (August 8, 1941 – May 31, 2009) was an American physician from Wichita, Kansas. He gained national attention as the medical director of Women's Health Care Services, which was one of the few abortion clinics nationwide at the time which provided late termination of pregnancy. Tiller was frequently targeted with protests and violence by anti-abortion groups and individuals. His clinic was firebombed in 1986 and, in 1993, Tiller was shot in both arms by anti-abortion extremist Shelley Shannon; she was sentenced to 23 years in prison and was released in 2018. On May 31, 2009, Tiller was fatally shot in the side of the head by anti-abortion extremist Scott Roeder while Tiller served as an usher during the Sunday morning service at his church in Wichita. Roeder was convicted of murder on January 29, 2010, and sentenced to life imprisonment.

[42] Just before 1 p.m. on June 10, 2009, 88-year-old James Wenneker von Brunn entered the United States Holocaust Memorial Museum in Washington, D.C. with a rifle and fatally shot Museum Special Police Officer Stephen Tyrone Johns. Other security guards returned fire, wounding von Brunn.

Von Brunn, a white supremacist, Holocaust denier and neo-Nazi, was charged with first-degree murder and firearms violations in federal court on June 11, 2009. On July 29, 2009, von Brunn was indicted by a federal grand jury on seven counts, including four which made him eligible for the death penalty; the charges included hate crime counts. On January 6, 2010, von Brunn died of natural causes while awaiting trial.

[43] Johnny Reid Edwards (born June 10, 1953) is an American lawyer and former politician who served as a U.S. senator from North Carolina. He was the Democratic nominee for vice president in 2004 alongside John Kerry, losing to incumbents George W. Bush and Dick Cheney. He also was a candidate for the Democratic presidential nomination in 2004 and 2008.

[44] Janet Ann Napolitano (born November 29, 1957) is an American politician, lawyer, and university administrator who served as the 21st Governor of Arizona from 2003 to 2009 and third U. S. Secretary of Homeland Security from 2009 to 2013, under President Barack Obama. She was named president of the University of California system in September 2013, and stepped down from that position on August 1, 2020 to join the faculty at Berkeley's Goldman School of Public Policy.

[45] Osama bin Mohammed bin Awad bin Laden (March 10, 1957 – May 2, 2011) was one of the founders of the pan-Islamic militant organization al-Qaeda. The group is designated as a terrorist group by the United Nations Security Council, the North Atlantic Treaty Organization (NATO), the European Union, and various countries. Bin Laden is mostly known for his role in masterminding the September 11 attacks, which resulted in the deaths of nearly 3,000 and prompted the United States (under President George W. Bush) to initiate the War on Terror.

[46] "Kilroy was here" was a meme that became popular during World War II, typically seen in graffiti. Its origin is debated, but the phrase and the accompanying doodle became associated with GIs in the 1940s: a bald-headed man with a prominent nose peeking over a wall with his fingers clutching the wall.

[47] The Terri Schiavo case was a euthanasia legal case in the United States that stretched from 1998 to 2005, involving Theresa Marie Schiavo (December 3, 1963 – March 31, 2005), a woman in an irreversible persistent vegetative state. Schiavo's husband and legal guardian argued that Schiavo would not have wanted prolonged artificial life support without the prospect of recovery, and in 1998 elected to remove her feeding tube. Schiavo's parents disputed her husband's assertions and challenged Schiavo's medical diagnosis, arguing in favor of continuing artificial nutrition and hydration. The highly publicized ordeal eventually involved state and federal politicians up to the level of President George W. Bush before Schiavo's feeding tube was ultimately removed.

[48] Michael DeWayne Brown (born November 8, 1954) served as the first undersecretary of Emergency Preparedness and Response, a division of the Department of Homeland Security. The post is generally referred to as the director or administrator of the Federal Emergency Management Agency (FEMA). Brown was appointed in January 2003 by President George W. Bush and resigned following his controversial handling of Hurricane Katrina in September 2005.

[49] Hurricane Katrina was a massive Category 5 Atlantic hurricane that caused over 1,800 deaths and $125 billion in damage in late August 2005, particularly in the

city of New Orleans and the surrounding areas. At the time, it was the costliest tropical cyclone on record and is now tied with 2017's Hurricane Harvey. The storm was the twelfth tropical cyclone, the fifth hurricane, and the third major hurricane of the 2005 Atlantic hurricane season, as well as the fourth-most intense Atlantic hurricane on record to make landfall in the contiguous United States.

[50] Halliburton Company is an American multinational corporation and one of the world's largest oil field service companies. It has operations in more than seventy countries, and owns hundreds of subsidiaries, affiliates, branches, brands and divisions worldwide. It employs over 50,000 people.

Halliburton has dual headquarters located in Houston and in Dubai, but it remains incorporated in the United States.

Halliburton has been involved in numerous controversies, including its connection with Dick Cheney—as U.S. Secretary of Defense, then CEO of the company, then Vice President of the United States—and the Iraq War, and the Deepwater Horizon, for which it agreed to settle outstanding legal claims against it by paying litigants $1.1 billion.

[51] Alexander Valterovich Litvinenko (August 30, 1962 or December 4, 1962 – 23 November 2006) was a British-naturalized Russian defector and former officer of the Russian Federal Security Service (FSB) who specialized in fighting organized crime. In November 1998, Litvinenko and other FSB officers publicly accused their superiors of ordering the assassination of the Russian oligarch Boris Berezovsky. Litvinenko was arrested the following March on charges of exceeding the authority of his position. He was acquitted in November 1999 but re-arrested before the charges were again dismissed in 2000. He fled with his family to London and was granted asylum in the United Kingdom, where he worked as a journalist, writer and consultant for the British intelligence services. During his time in Boston, Lincolnshire, Litvinenko wrote two books, *Blowing Up Russia: Terror from Within* and *Lubyanka Criminal Group*, wherein he accused the Russian secret services of staging the Russian apartment bombings in 1999 and other acts of terrorism in an effort to bring Vladimir Putin to power. He also accused Putin of ordering the assassination of a female Russian journalist in 2006. On November 1, 2006, Litvinenko suddenly fell ill and was hospitalized in what was established as a case of polonium-210 poisoning. Litvinenko died from the poisoning on November 23, 2006. He became the first known victim of lethal polonium 210-induced acute radiation syndrome.

[52] Simba is the protagonist of Disney's *The Lion King* franchise. Introduced in the 1994 film *The Lion King*, Walt Disney Animation's 32nd animated feature, the character later appears in *The Lion King II: Simba's Pride* (1998) and *The Lion King 1½* (2004) as well as a 2019 remake of the original film.

[53] Anne Sexton (November 9, 1928 – October 4, 1974) was an American poet known for her extremely personal, confessional verse. She won the Pulitzer Prize for poetry in 1967 for her book *Live or Die*.

[54] In early July 2010, former Republican vice-presidential candidate Sarah Palin went on Sean Hannity's *Fox News* show and called for the Obamas (President Barack Obama and his wife, Michelle) to "refudiate" statements representatives of the NAACP had made about racist elements in the Tea Party. Refudiate was not a word then, but it is now. Palin combined "refute" with "repudiate" and won a spot in the dictionary. In fact, that November the *New Oxford American Dictionary* named "refudiate," its 2010 Word of the Year.

[55] Galileo di Vincenzo Bonaiuti de' Galilei (February 15, 1564 – January 8, 1642) was an Italian astronomer, physicist and engineer, sometimes described as a polymath, from Pisa. Galileo has been called the "father of observational astronomy," the "father of modern physics," the "father of the scientific method" and the "father of modern science." Galileo studied speed and velocity, gravity and free fall, the principle of relativity, inertia, projectile motion and also worked in applied science and technology, describing the properties of pendulums and "hydrostatic balances." He invented the thermoscope and various military compasses, and used the telescope for scientific observations of celestial objects. Galileo's championing of Copernican heliocentrism (the theory that the Earth rotates daily and revolves around the sun yearly) was met with opposition by the Catholic Church and some astronomers. The matter was investigated by the Roman Inquisition in 1615, and it concluded that heliocentrism was absurd and heretical since it contradicted Holy Scripture. Galileo later defended his views in *Dialogue Concerning the Two Chief World Systems* (1632), which appeared to attack Pope Urban VIII and thus alienated both the Pope and the Jesuits, who had supported him up until this point. Galileo was tried by the Inquisition, found "vehemently suspect of heresy," and forced to recant. He spent the remainder of his life under house arrest.

[56] Condoleezza Rice (born November 14, 1954) is an American diplomat, political scientist, civil servant, and professor who is the current director of the Hoover Institution at Stanford University. Rice served as the 66th United States Secretary of State from 2005 to 2009 and as the 20th United States National Security Advisor from 2001 to 2005. A member of the Republican Party, Rice was the first female African-American secretary of state and the first woman to serve as National Security Advisor. Until the election of Barack Obama as president in 2008, Rice and her predecessor, Colin Powell, were the highest-ranking African Americans in the history of the federal executive branch (by virtue of the secretary of state standing fourth in the presidential line of succession).

[57] H. Norman Schwarzkopf Jr. (August 22, 1934 – December 27, 2012) was a United States Army general, know chiefly for serving as the commander of United States Central Command during the 1991 Gulf War.

[58] Grover Glenn Norquist (born October 19, 1956) is a Republican political activist and tax reduction advocate who is the founder and president of Americans for Tax Reform, an organization that opposes all tax increases. He is the primary promoter of the Taxpayer Protection Pledge, a pledge signed by lawmakers who agree to oppose increases in marginal income tax rates for individuals and businesses, as well as net reductions or eliminations of deductions and credits without a matching reduced tax rate.

[59] Samuel Joseph Wurzelbacher (born December 3, 1973), known as "Joe the Plumber," is an American conservative activist and commentator. He garnered international attention during the 2008 U.S. presidential election when, during a videotaped campaign stop in Ohio by then Democratic nominee Senator Barack Obama, Wurzelbacher raised concerns that Obama's tax policy would increase taxes on small business owners. The McCain–Palin campaign brought him along to make several appearances in campaign events in Ohio and McCain often referenced "Joe the Plumber" in campaign speeches and in the final presidential debate, as a metaphor for middle-class Americans. In 2012, Wurzelbacher ran on the Republican ticket to represent Ohio's 9th congressional district in the House of Representatives, losing to Democratic incumbent Marcy Kaptur.

[60] John Alexander Graves III (August 6, 1920 – July 31, 2013) was a Texas writer best known for *Goodbye to a River*, an American classic published in 1960.

[61] The Baby boomers (often shortened to Boomers) are the generation following the Silent Generation and preceding Generation X. The group is generally defined as people born from 1946 to 1964, during the post–World War II baby boom.

[62] Michael Francis Moore (born April 23, 1954) is a progressive documentary filmmaker, author, and activist. His works frequently address the topics of globalization and capitalism. Moore won the 2002 Academy Award for Best Documentary Feature for *Bowling for Columbine*, which examined the causes of the Columbine High School massacre and American gun culture. He also directed and produced *Fahrenheit 9/11*, a critical look at the presidency of George W. Bush and the War on Terror, which earned $119,194,771 to become the highest-grossing American documentary of all time. The film also won the Palme d'Or at the 2004 Cannes film festival.

[63] Keith Theodore Olbermann (born January 27, 1959) is an American sports and political commentator and writer.

[64] Randolph Silliman Bourne (May 30, 1886 – December 22, 1918) was a progressive writer and intellectual born in Bloomfield, New Jersey, and a graduate of Columbia University. He is considered to be a spokesman for young American

radicals living during World War I. His articles appeared in journals including *The Seven Arts* and *The New Republic.*

[65] John Sidney McCain III (August 29, 1936 – August 25, 2018) was an American politician, statesman and United States Navy officer (and Vietnam veteran) who served as a United States Senator for Arizona from 1987 until his death in 2018. He previously served two terms in the United States House of Representatives and was the Republican nominee for president of the United States in the 2008 election, which he lost to Barack Obama.

[66] In the context of the Iraq War, "The Surge" refers to President George W. Bush's 2007 increase in the number of American troops in order to provide security to Baghdad and Al Anbar Governorate.

[67] The Ogallala Aquifer is a shallow water table aquifer surrounded by sand, silt, clay and gravel located beneath the Great Plains in the United States. One of the world's largest aquifers, it underlies an area of approximately 174,000 square miles in portions of eight states (Texas, New Mexico, Colorado, Oklahoma, Nebraska, Kansas, South Dakota and Wyoming. The aquifer is part of the High Plains Aquifer System, and resides in the Ogallala Formation, which is the principal geologic unit underlying eighty percent of the High Plains

[68] *Citizens United v. Federal Election Commission*, 558 U.S. 310 (2010), was a landmark decision of the U. S. Supreme Court concerning the relationship between campaign finance and free speech. The Court held that the free speech clause of the First Amendment prohibits the government from restricting secret, independent expenditures for political campaigns by corporations, wealthy billionaires, and committees established for the purpose of fundraising (PACs).

[69] Jack Allan Abramoff (born February 28, 1959) is a Republican lobbyist, businessman, film producer, writer, and convicted felon. Abramoff was at the center of an extensive corruption investigation that resulted in his conviction and to twenty-one people either pleading guilty or being found guilty, including Bush White House officials J. Steven Griles and David Safavian, U.S. Representative Bob Ney, and nine other lobbyists and congressional aides.

[70] I. Lewis "Scooter" Libby (born August 22, 1950) is an American lawyer and former adviser to Vice President Dick Cheney. From 2001 to 2005, Libby held the offices of Assistant to the Vice President for National Security Affairs, Chief of Staff to the Vice President of the United States, and Assistant to the President during the administration of George W. Bush. In October 2005, Libby resigned from all three government positions after he was indicted on five counts by a federal grand jury concerning the investigation of the leak of the covert identity of Central Intelligence Agency officer Valerie Plame Wilson. He was convicted of four counts (one count of obstruction of justice, two counts of perjury, and one count of making false statements), making him the highest-ranking White House official

convicted in a government scandal since John Poindexter, the national security adviser to President Ronald Reagan during the Iran–Contra affair.

[71] Friedrich Wilhelm Nietzsche (October 15, 1844 – August 25, 1900) was a German philosopher, cultural critic, composer, poet, writer, and philologist whose work has exerted a profound influence on modern intellectual history. He began his career as a classical philologist before turning to philosophy. At the age of twenty-four, he became the youngest person ever to hold the Chair of Classical Philology at the University of Basel. Nietzsche resigned in 1879 due to health problems, completed much of his core writing in the following decade. In 1889, at age forty-four, he suffered a collapse and afterward a complete loss of his mental faculties. He lived his remaining years in the care of his mother until her death in 1897 and then with his sister Elisabeth Förster-Nietzsche. Nietzsche died in 1900.

[72] *Twilight of the Idols, or, How to Philosophize with a Hammer* was written by Friedrich Nietzsche in 1888, and published in 1889.

[73] Bristol Sheeran Marie Palin (born October 18, 1990) is an American public speaker, reality television personality, and real estate agent. She is the oldest daughter and second of five children of Todd and Sarah Palin. Sarah Palin is a former governor of Alaska and was a Republican vice-presidential candidate in the 2008 election.